FOOD & BOOZE

A *Tin House* Literary Feast

FOOD &

BOOZE

Essays and Recipes

Foreword by Michelle Wildgen

Illustrations by Nicole J. Georges

TinHouseBooks

Published by Tin House Books, Portland, Oregon,
and New York, New York
Distributed to the trade by Publishers Group West,
1700 Fourth St., Berkeley, CA 94710, www.pgw.com

ISBN 0-9773127-7-1

First U.S. edition 2006

Cover and interior design by Laura Shaw, Inc.

www.tinhouse.com

CONTENTS

Foreword / MICHELLE WILDGEN — 7

Food / GRACE PALEY — 12

Ode to a Martini / ELISSA SCHAPPELL — 14

My Soul Upon the Grill / STEVE ALMOND — 24

Eating Fish Alone / LYDIA DAVIS — 37

Notes from the Nauseous / CARLA SPARTOS — 47

Dinner with the Borgias / LISA GROSSMAN — 55

The Lotus-Eaters / JEFF KOEHLER — 71

Becherovka / FRANCINE PROSE — 84

The Apple of Their Eyes / SARA PERRY — 91

Ode to an Egg / MICHELLE WILDGEN — 108

Here's to Crime! / DAVID LEHMAN — 120

Yellowtail / STUART DYBEK — 131

Mezcal / MARK STATMAN — 140

The Path of Righteousness / MATTHEW BATT — 149

The Green Fairy / ELISSA SCHAPPELL   166

Persian Cuisine / SHUSHA GUPPY   181

My Life with Sukiyaki / ANTHONY SWOFFORD   202

Rummy / A. J. RATHBUN   213

Beating the Heat / RICH KING   223

Drinking My Inheritance / SARA ROAHEN   232

A Season in Elk Country / LYNNE SAMPSON   243

Up Your Goose with a Boneless Duck / CHRIS OFFUTT   258

The Taste of a Wild Mushroom / EUGENIA BONE   267

The End of Laughter / LAN SAMANTHA CHANG   286

In a Crowded Kitchen / HEATHER HARTLEY   294

FOREWORD

Food has always had its place in literature. While a meal might reflect class or temperament, it can betray deeper truths as well. Every writer knows that a character eating and drinking is a character unguarded, a character indulging or denying hungers. Who could omit such a potent tool for creating a fictional landscape?

Yet in real life, kitchens and their cooks were once secreted as far away as possible from the drawing room. If you arrived at a friend's for dinner in the nineteenth century, no rich scents greeted you. With the fragrance of roast goose and pudding kept politely at bay, diners could ignore such an ignominious need as hunger until they sat down at the table. (Even then it was bad form to be famished.) By the time the meal made its way through cramped hallways in the hands of a downtrodden servant, the food had cooled to room temperature and an acceptable scentlessness. The point was not that meals must be cold and bland, but to show that the host had enough money, space, and servants to keep food in its proper place: hidden until the proper moment.

Now, of course, guests would be impolite not to praise (and a bit worried not to detect) whatever dinner scents fill the house. Magazines teem with suggestions for making the kitchen the most comfortable gathering spot in the home. To the delight of the editors at *Tin House*, the kitchen has swelled, metaphorically speaking, to encompass the living room, the sitting room—maybe even the bedroom; we can't know everything about our readers—and, best of all, the library.

~~~~~~~~~~~~~~~~~~~~~~~~~~~~~~

It's a given that dining in the United States has become more global, thoughtful, pretentious, enjoyed, and agonized over in the last half century or so. Some of us may have been born too late for the Julia Child revolution in the early sixties, but we can recall puzzling over the word *shiitake* in the early eighties. The food sections of newspapers still include the usual quick 'n' easy recipes, and the gourmets are still swirling wine around their mouths and carping on the traits of a proper foie gras mousse, but there are also millions trying both, and everything in between. The joy of serious writers covering food is their ability to see the significant in all of those possibilities: to find the tension in the uneaten plate of vegetables, the pleasures in a bowl of potato chips, and the novelty and discovery in the labor over an elaborate dish from another country.

A crossover has happened: open a glossy food mag and there are the poets and novelists, chatting away about mangoes, *boudin blanc*, oysters. It makes sense, just as it does for a literary magazine to feature food and drink writing. From the beginning, *Tin House* has asked writers to talk about food and booze in our Readable Feast and Blithe Spirits departments:

who else is trained to tease out every detail of a sensation like hunger or flavor, and to ponder its meaning in the most offbeat, funniest, or saddest way? And for the writers, it's pleasure; it's sensual. It's a chance to enjoy the community and the delights of a meal even when sitting at a computer, alone, as they so often are. Food, in other words, busted out of the scullery and the dinner party got a hell of a lot more fun.

~~~~~~~~~~~~~~~~~~~~~~~~~~~~

Attend a dinner party at *Tin House*, and you'll find we're enthusiastic but democratic consumers. We ask writers about the meals they've loved and the cocktails they can't forget, as well as the ones they wish they could. The answers are invariably far more fascinating and diverse than we ever could have dreamed. We've devoured essays hailing the silvery charms of a martini and the heavy-bottomed, spicy glug of a Wisconsin-style old-fashioned. We followed Matthew Batt's tortured, comic road to serious sourdough bread as readily as we dove after Stuart Dybek in pursuit of a yellowtail snapper, the voice of Castro murmuring recipes in our sea-clogged ears the whole way there. We might have guessed that Steve Almond would feel passionately, but we never would have guessed that passion extends to chicken salad. We stand corrected. We learned that the denizens of Lynne Sampson's tiny Oregon town morph into hunters and hoarders every elk season. Grace Paley responded to our queries with a taut, tart, and mournful poem on lost youth and takeout shrimp. Lydia Davis gave us the low-down on the idiosyncrasies of dining alone, dining thought-fully, dining on sardine sandwiches. It turns out that Francine Prose flew home from Prague with an esoteric-liqueur habit that may or may not be medicinal and that Elissa Schappell has curbed but not quite kicked her treacherous love of absinthe. We understand. We're not too into what's good for us, either.

So we too dally in Hell's Kitchen and snap awake with a frothy, eggy, booze-laced eye-opener. And we support A. J. Rathbun in his doomed but noble quest to bring back the colo-nial American practice of childhood rum drinking. No topic is off-limits, too strange, or too dangerous, as evidenced by the treatise on the poisonous dining habits of the Borgias. (A tip: Don't take your eyes off the pope's fat, hollow ring when he pauses near your glass of wine.) We've never gotten our hands on Homer's much dreamed-of lotus fruit, but Jeff Koehler did, and it damn near claimed him, too. Also, we discovered there's a reason that squirrel casserole tastes so much like chicken.

Yet life, and *Food & Booze*, is not only about the arcane or the bizarre. Our writers find the story in the familiar as well. They see the ordinary from the slight angle of the outsider, and suddenly the customary fare is transformed: puffed up with secrets and history, light shining through the skin. Fam-ily—scattered or close, hungry or sated—lurks in stories of apple pie, Persian rice, the humble egg, and the meaty wild mushroom. The love affair that never quite happened turns out to be as bittersweet in a Greek diner as it would be in the

French Laundry, while the affair that did rushes back with the fragrance of homemade *gyoza*.

Therefore we're skeptical when the occasional writer insists he has nothing to tell us about eating and drinking. We know that even the ones hunched over a laptop, spooning peanut butter from the jar, can discourse on the merits of plastic versus silver spoons, crunchy versus smooth. And we can't wait to try their recipes.

—*Michelle Wildgen*

Food

GRACE PALEY

My friend who's ninety-two said sighed
oh Grace there's not much left when
your time comes you'll see wait I
forgot at least there's ice cream

meanwhile she lives on baked beans and
chocolate milk plans letters to the local
papers I know it's too late now
eat shit you bastards

my other friend who's forty-one sardonically
asked now is it true you've given up
dead cow for cabbage yes yes why not
it's years since that self-satisfied old
fertility goddess has pestered me
for blood

thirty-five years before he died
my dear friend's son in childhood's despair
picked up his second grade lunch box
oh ma is it sardines again?

then lived his life almost to the end
and one day in the hospital oh ma
go down to St. Mark's Place you'll find
a tiny restaurant called Chin's ask
for Tien's rice and shrimp then if
for once you've got it right
I'll eat it

Ode to a Martini

ELISSA SCHAPPELL

One must always be drunk. . . . To avoid that horrible burden of Time grabbing your shoulders and crushing you to earth, you must get drunk without restraint. But on what? On wine, poetry or virtue, whatever you fancy. But get drunk.

—CHARLES BAUDELAIRE

There is scarcely a glee club, bridge group, or rugby team that doesn't have its own signature drink—a potation that binds them as a tribe. For some it's bowls of creamy cocoa warmed with a heating pad, or orange juice on ice goosed with a bit of Stoli, or a pony keg foaming Old Milwaukee. For *Tin House* it is the martini. Is it any wonder?

Sure, we could have chosen a fizz, a rickey, or an Angel's Kiss. Certainly the *Tin House* Pousse Café had a certain soigné charm. The cosmopolitan and sidecar were likewise bandied about, but we *all* love martinis. Gin martinis. None of this vodka-come-lately business. We demand gin, the Mother of Ruin. How could one not embrace the martini as the ultimate cocktail? The martini is both grail and lodestone. Its literary lineage is impeccable, from Jack London to W. Somerset Maugham to Ernest Hemingway. Pick up Barnaby Conrad's *The Martini* (which I've cribbed from unmercifully) for an exhaustive and colorful history of all the artistic and political folderol swirling around the martini.

In essence, a martini is like a kiss; anyone can make one, but a good one takes your breath.

And like a kiss, you never forget your first one.

Mine was at the 21 Club. I was just twenty-one and on a job interview for a lowly position at a highly regarded monthly magazine. At the first opportunity, the editor I was lunching with, a silver-haired gentleman sporting discreet gold cuff links the size of almonds, flagged a waiter and ordered a martini, and I, of course, followed suit. I felt just like Myrna Loy as Nora Charles in *The Thin Man*. If I squinted, couldn't this gentleman be William Powell? The food was ghastly, the interview worse, but the martini was heaven, and after the second I scarcely cared when the gentleman dropped his hand onto my knee and told me I reminded him of his daughter. Needless to say, the job was not to be, but I fell head over cocktail shakers for martinis.

Martinis were emblematic of who I'd come to New York to be. My literary heroes drank them, or at least the characters in their books did. There was always someone with a perfect profile bellying up to the bar in the stories of F. Scott Fitzgerald and John Cheever. And then of course there was Dorothy Parker, whom I liked to imagine at the Algonquin, saying for the first time:

I like to have a martini
Two at the very most—
After three I'm under the table,
After four I'm under my host.

And Robert Benchley—who liked his martinis with "just enough vermouth to take away that nasty, watery look"—nearly toppling out of his chair with glee.

Even when I was poor and living on pickles and saltines in the Village, I drank martinis. Especially when I was poor I drank martinis. Alone in my freezer were a bottle of gin, two martini glasses, and some batteries for the radio. Martinis sustained me. How bad could life be if one still had martinis?

Martinis were a shot in the arm. Hip, hip kiddo. Things are going to be looking up soon. That old phone is going to leap off the hook!

New Yorker writer E. B. White boasted that he drank martinis "the way other people take aspirin," and referred to his pet cocktail as "the elixir of quietude."

The first sip of a martini is, to my mind, one of the greatest kicks in the pants around. The second sip is bracing; it makes me feel brave, hopeful even. On the third I sigh.

After one martini you start calling up friends to get a party afoot. After two you are solving the world's problems on the back of a cocktail napkin, and by the third—which is the absolute limit—you are undone. Which is not to say that a girl couldn't rifle a high-heeled shoe at a boy who isn't paying her the proper attention.

To Wit: it does seem that the incidence of fisticuffs when one is in one's juniper cups is particularly high. I have it on good authority that a woman who has been tossing back martinis is far more likely to slap the face of a badly behaved man than a woman who has been drinking, say, rum and Diet Coke. Boorish behavior goes almost unnoticed by the docile rum-and-Coke drinker—if it does crease her gentle mind she might giggle, or toss her hair. Certainly we *don't condone* all this drama, all this circuslike carrying on. We like to watch it, yes, but condone? Absolutely Not.

The morning after a martini bout, the old saying "Martinis are like breasts—one is not enough and three is too many" springs ever so delicately (oh, the suffering) to mind.

The history of the martini is oft-debated. Was the martini born in San Francisco and originally baptized the Martinez, or was it a bartender at the Knickerbocker Hotel in midtown Manhattan who can rightly claim parentage? Frankly, I don't care. What is indisputable is that the martini is a uniquely American cocktail. H. L. Mencken declared the martini "the only American invention as perfect as a sonnet." And American also is the compulsion to improve on the tried and true martini recipe, endlessly. A staggering number of cocktailers are gaily flirting with martinis dosed with the essence of Chanel No. 5, sour apple, and Bazooka Joe. While at the far end of the bar sits the purist, a salted peanut clutched to his breast. His poison? The Olive Twist Martini, the antithesis of these gaudy imbibitions, offering as it does neither olive nor twist.

Perhaps it is not uniquely American, but it is certainly a fact that most martini drinkers, given half a chance, will preach endlessly about the perfect formula. Oh, if only all the mysteries of life, both light and dark, could be broken down into such keen mathematical formulas, a pony of this, a jigger of that, two fingers of tolerance, a dash of devil-may-care!

Rarely does one have to tease the recipe out of a martini genius. It's offered in a sonorous baritone like the word of God, or the great Harry Craddock himself. *It's imperative to rinse the shaker or glass with vermouth*—this is called the "in-and-out" method. *It's a scandal to use anything but British gin.*

"To provoke, or sustain, a reverie in a bar," said filmmaker Luis Buñuel, director of *The Discreet Charm of the Bourgeoisie,* "you have to drink English gin, especially in the form of a dry martini."

In the year 2000, style dictates that the drier the martini is, the better. It wasn't always so. *The Savoy Cocktail Book* of the 1930s, recently reissued—which many consider the Rosetta Stone of cocktail books—suggests a dry martini cocktail be one-third French vermouth, two-thirds dry gin, shaken well and strained into glasses. A medium martini cocktail calls for one-quarter French vermouth, one-quarter Italian vermouth, and one-half dry gin, shaken well and strained into glasses.

Much has been made of the vermouth. Italian or French? How much, how little? According to Winston Churchill, to achieve the proper measure of vermouth one need only glance across the room at the vermouth bottle. The esteemed poet and accomplished martini craftsman William Wadsworth advocates the "dirty martini" of FDR, which uses the in-and-out method, with just the faintest splash of the olive's brine added.

Ah, but what of the garnishments? In the name of tradition, sanity, and good taste we consider only two truly worthy. There is the brilliant twist of lemon—which imparts the loveliest iridescent sheen to the drink's icy surface, the ribbon of yellow rind so like a streamer. Or there is the classic green olive, stuffed with a cheeky pimiento, resting on the bottom of the glass like sunken treasure. One might want to take into account, when pondering twist versus olive, that *Winesburg, Ohio* author Sherwood Anderson died from peritonitis after swallowing the toothpick from a martini olive. Certainly this shouldn't sway one's judgment, but I couldn't in good conscience keep that to myself.

The debate about who penned the immortal line "I must get out of these wet clothes and into a dry martini" (Robert Benchley, Alexander Woollcott, or Mae West?) is heated, but it is nothing compared to the fracas that arises when discussing whether to shake or to stir.

Joan Crawford, for one, demanded her martinis be stirred. I know I speak for a veritable horde of agitating bartenders when I insist that a martini must be shaken.

The knock against shaking is that it "bruises" the gin. Perhaps it does, but my palate certainly can't discern such a corruption, and who is to say it isn't the bruising that gives the gin that extra splendor? Bruise away, I say. To my mind, a good martini is all in the shaking. Shaking is foreplay. One must shake and shake and shake until one's fingers go numb and freeze to the shaker's frosty surface. Then, and only then, is she ready.

Ernest Hemingway, whose fondness for arctic blondes was perhaps surpassed only by his fondness for ice-cold Gibsons, described his mixology method in a letter to a friend:

We have found a way of making ice in the deep freeze in tennis ball tubes that come out 14 degrees below zero and with glasses frozen too makes the coldest martini in the world. Just enough vermouth to cover the bottom of the glass, ¾ ounce of gin, and the Spanish cocktail onions very crisp and also 14 degrees below zero when they go into the glass.

As long as there are martini drinkers the spirit of innovation lives, a boozy muse blowing into your ear. In our case, the angel of inspiration graced us with her presence a scant three hours before our premiere party, and (ahem) inquired politely after the specialty of the house. The Tin House. Thus, in a fit of whimsy, and enflamed by the provocative percussion on the hi-fi, we set out to create the first Tin House Martini.

First we dashed four ounces of ice-cold Bombay Sapphire Gin into a martini shaker piled with ice, then tipped in a thimbleful of Noilly Pratt, and began to shake our darling in a syncopated fashion—as though we were marathon dance partners—until we were ready to drop. Once the room stopped spinning, we poured and garnished our baby with a blackberry. Now if we had been out in Portland, in the West Coast office, we could have had the pièce de résistance of berries, the marionberry, but no, we were trapped in Manhattan, so for us poor stiffs, the fat blackberry sufficed quite nicely.

I don't imagine I have to tell you how popular this drink was. Only now are we back on friendly terms with the neighbors. Personally, I adore it. Blue aromatic gin, a purple berry to stain your lips . . .

But there is always room for improvement, and devoted as we are to the quest for the perfect Tin House Martini—and spurred by a concern about the year-round availability of first-rate produce, not to mention the demands of our publisher, who is rarely if ever completely satisfied—we soldiered on. Grueling, grueling work.

It wasn't until divine providence delivered us Greg Connolly, a bartender at the Four Seasons restaurant in Manhattan, that we found a man—no, a martini genius—who could concoct a martini worthy of the glittering mantle: the Tin House Martini.

You know that we'd love to have each and every one of you in for a round, but until that time comes—say, when our neighbors go to the Hamptons for the summer—please feel free to play with our recipe, or demand, nay, educate—no, no, *enlighten*—your local bartender to the charms of the Tin House Martini.

RECIPE

The Tin House Martini

Pour ½ ounce of Pernod into a cocktail shaker and swirl until it coats the inside of the shaker; pour off any excess. In countries where it is still legal, such as Portugal and Spain, absinthe can be appropriately substituted for Pernod.

Splash 2 eye-dropperfuls of Cinzano dry vermouth into the bottom of the shaker, and again swirl it about, then pour off the excess.

Pour 4 to 4 ½ ounces of Tangueray gin into the shaker, add ice, and with a ridiculously long-handled silver mixing spoon, stir exactly twenty times.

Pour the drink into a very well-chilled martini glass, then add 3 small cocktail olives, or 2 large ones, sans toothpick.

The flavors of olive and Pernod commingle so deliciously that at least one of the olives should be consumed after the drink is finished. You see, sometimes consolation *can* be found in the bottom of a martini glass.

My Soul Upon the Grill

A NOT-SO-BRIEF INQUIRY INTO THE OBSESSIVE ORIGINS OF A SINGLE RECIPE

STEVE ALMOND

To fully appreciate the recipe in question—a recipe that I have inflicted, almost unremittingly, on anyone I have met over the last five years—I will first need to discuss several ancillary topics, including (but not limited to) *the marinade, grill conduct, my failed vegetarianism,* and *the experience of the world in my mouth.*

In the beginning, God created the marinade

My First Law of Marinades—there are only two—is that a true marinade does not come from a book. It does not come from a TV chef with a marketable accent. It does not come from a friend. It comes from within. It evolves, organically, from the life of the person for whom the marinade has, in some deeply existential sense, been waiting. In my own nomenclature, the *marinadee.*

So let us consider how the marinade in question came about. We must begin with breakfast, my favorite meal of the day, and my move to Boston, where, for the first time in my life, I experienced the singular pleasure of real maple syrup. It will go without saying that the central allure of breakfast is the chance to combine, with some measure of dignity, smoked meats and buttery starches drenched in maple syrup.

I should note here that the central driving impulse of my palate is not toward sugar (as I had long felt sure) or salt (as I had recently begun to suspect) but toward the simultaneous, legitimized consumption of both, what I call the *Salt-Sugar Nexus*.

My original marinade consisted of syrup, soy sauce, and a little garlic powder. It was, well, *adequate*, which is another word for tragically insufficient in the realm of true passion. The soy sauce was too harsh for the subtle alchemy I hoped to achieve. I made the switch to teriyaki. I was drawn not so much to the latent sweetness as to the tang of fermentation at the heart of the teriyaki flavor gestalt.

There were other, less calculated, modifications. At a certain point, in an effort to temper the redolence of the garlic, I started adding sesame oil to the mix. But then, as often happens when you use as much sesame oil as I do, I ran out. I drove to the store to get more, but they were out. "We got seeds," said the kid unhappily charged with overseeing the spice shelf. "You know, the kind like you get on a bun."

So I sprinkled half the bottle onto my pan full of chicken. It did not look promising. It looked, if I may be frank, like my chicken had lice. But on the grill, something magical happened: the sesame seeds, affixed to the chicken by means of the syrup, released their vital oils to the marinade.

This brings us to the Second Law of Marinades, which is that true marinades must be forged in the sweat of the grill (let us put aside, for the sake of not embarrassing me, whether one can forge anything in sweat), meaning profound, chemical transformations must take place.

The central example of this would be the maple syrup itself, which caramelizes on the grill, producing that sweet, burned taste so familiar to lovers of crème brûlée and glazed ham. It was true of the sesame seeds, as well. The flames awakened their essence, toasted them to a golden crunch.

I might have stopped here, yes, of course. But my approach to cooking—an approach I would characterize as somewhere between transcendental and incoherent—requires innovation. In this case, I had a marinade with an *ideal binding viscosity*.

Anyone who cooks with garlic (and I'm mistrustful of anyone who doesn't) realizes the attendant dangers: a sharp, aromatic flavor that can dominate an entire meal and render subsequent foreplay difficult. *Roasted* garlic, however, mellows into something closer to an herbal accent. And I'm pleased to report that roasted garlic combined with caramelized maple sugar, teriyaki, and toasted sesame seeds produces what I have referred to elsewhere as a mouthgasm.

I did try a few other ingredients—a grainy Dijon mustard, a jigger of red wine, a pinch of chipotle-based dry rub. The results were not disastrous. The flavors merely competed.

This, too, is a vital lesson in the realm of the marinade, not quite a law, maybe closer to a corollary: the tongue must be delighted, not confused.

A few words about the grill

I am not one of those guys who spends hours pontificating on the mandates of the grill, who lays down a small fortune accessorizing, who pants over the relevant grill-porn from Restoration Hardware and wields the spatula as if it were an instrument of war. I am considerably worse.

Specifically, I've developed certain spiritual ideas, emotional biases, what my analyst would term—if I ever spoke to him about the grill, which I do not—an ideological fetish.

It begins like this: Human beings are inexorably drawn toward fire, which has, for most of our formative evolution as a species, been the fundamental source of warmth, safety, and nutritional gratification. Stoves are, in the grand scheme of things, an infantile domestic prop. (I shall not even begin to express my contempt for microwaves.)

The sensual signifiers of fire—the orange snap of the flames, the smell and taste of the smoke—are hardwired. It is for this reason that cooking over a fire, which most of the world still does, triggers certain vestigial limbic impulses, in my case a desire to lick tendrils of grease from the grill.

As to equipment, I use a portable Weber Smokey Joe, which cost $29.99 when I purchased it, late last century. The grill surface is eighteen inches across and stands approximately fourteen inches off the ground, which means that I am forced—or rather, I choose—to hunch over the fire in a manner that has been described, by more than one friend, as "distinctly simian." This posture often causes me to suffer a minor and not entirely unpleasant case of smoke inhalation. I wear very little clothing while grilling, a pair of shorts at most, so my skin and hair will absorb the smoke.

There is certainly an argument to be made that the reason I haven't purchased a newer, snazzier grill is because I am cheap. Fine. But the real reason is that I believe each grill possesses a kind of soul, or that each grill, at least, captures something of the soul of the various pieces of flesh that have been cooked upon it, and that this contributes to an overall accrued capacity to bestow flavor. (Anyone with a favorite skillet will back me up on this one.)

It should go without saying that the use of a gas grill is verboten. It's not that gas corrupts the meat. It corrupts *the process*. And process is everything. For me, this means lighting the coals in a chimney—whatever brand you want, but no lighter fluid, please—and allowing them to turn an ashy gray before layering them beneath the grill. Next, you should liberally sprinkle wood chips that have been soaked in water for a minimum of half an hour. Mesquite will do fine in a pinch; hickory is the ideal. Immediately cover.

What you're attempting to create is a meat bong. That is, smoke must pass through the meat and, in so doing, some vital residue must remain in the meat.

Ah, yes, the meat.

For this recipe the only cut that will do is a boneless chicken thigh.

Thighs have a far richer natural flavor and succulence than the more popular chicken breast, yes, in part because they have more fat, *fine*, but also because they absorb flavor more effectively than any other meat medium I've encountered. (Please trust me on this. I've done the research.) What's more, the boneless thigh, if flattened and tenderized, offers a greater surface area than virtually any other cut of meat. And surface area is a crucial factor with this marinade, so as to maximize that sumptuous, caramelized crust.

In the question of how long one grills these thighs, let me quote the philosopher Epicurus, who is said to have pronounced to his acolytes, many marinades ago: *The spit, if properly tended, will sing to you.*

What did he mean by this? Epicurus has always struck me as a bit of a closet Sophist, so chances are he was just bullshitting. But to my mind, he was speaking about the auditory cues that are paramount when working with a live flame.

You will hear a lot of sizzling early on, as the excess fat burns off. I wait for the first pronounced silence before flipping. I also rotate the grill to offset the effect of any hot spots. Those truly neurotic about salmonella can always cut into the thickest piece. If all goes well, here is what you will see: a dark, shiny glaze around meat that has taken on a reddish tint. Don't be alarmed! This is just what you want.

There is nothing like meat straight from the grill—as it still retains most of its juices—and this recipe will call for an almost immediate dicing of the meat. But let us pause here, for a moment, to sample a single slice. Hold it close to your face. Note the flecks of garlic and golden sesame seeds captured, as if in amber. Now take a bite. What does that taste like? It tastes like maple-cured bacon.

If meat is murder, I am a serial killer

Not long ago, I made my fourth attempt to become a vegetarian. I did so for the obvious reasons. It is a healthier lifestyle. It is morally wrong to eat the flesh of animals, not just because animals have feelings—those who speak about the feelings of chickens, I suspect, have not spent much time with them; they are not a species that evinces much pity—but because the net energy required to supply me with a nice, hot chicken thigh would be better spent on, say, soybeans.

My veggie friends have urged me to try grilling veggie burgers, veggie dogs, tofu turkey, and the like. My objection here isn't to the ingredients, but to the artifice. My mouth knows meat, and it knows the stuff pretending, with a certain desperate do-gooderism, to be meat.

I need not detail the particulars of my most recent failure. For the record, it did not involve, as with attempts one and three, a bacon double cheeseburger from Burger King, or, as I prefer to think of it, the *Traif Deluxe*. Nor did it last especially long. I am going to estimate in the neighborhood of 121 hours.

I might blame some of this on the fact that meat—red meat, especially—was a rare treat during my upbringing. I can still remember the salivary frenzy provoked by my mother's London broil, prepared once a fortnight, and the manner in which I kept a silent but exact record of the number of slices consumed by each member of my family.

But the truth is, even if she'd gorged us on the finest cuts and chops, I would have been drawn to meat. My tongue is a cruel, blood-seeking radar, and my teeth lust for fibers of animal muscle.

It is for this very reason that my attitudes toward the marinade and the grill are so—*concerted*. I take it as a moral duty to prepare meat in a manner that will ensure the greatest taste per dead animal unit. So, for instance, I have been known to grill a kielbasa and to use this to create the stock for a supple black bean soup. Half a burger, when finely chopped and sautéed with garlic and a full pound of mushrooms, becomes the base for a sumptuous tomato sauce.

The idea is not to eliminate meat, but to make the most of its unique capacity for delivering flavor. I think of this as the First Law of Flavor Conservation.

In which the recipe is at last (at last!) revealed

It will have occurred to you, by now, that I am profoundly disturbed. Then again, most great recipes are the by-products of madness. (It was Goethe, of all people, who referred to the culinary arts as a form of "productive dementia.") And the recipe I'm about to detail is, I assure you, the greatest substance you will ever place in your mouth. It makes the Savoy truffle taste like dirt. It makes lobster bisque taste like snot.

I should mention the recipe in question is for chicken salad.

Now, I have eaten a good many chicken salads in my day and been disappointed by most of them—bland, awash in mayo, not fit for stale bread. This chicken salad, by contrast, has reduced skeptical foodies (is there any other kind?) to blubbering sycophants. Perhaps more to the point, it has gotten me chicks.

As with the marinade, the recipe is the result of deeply personal, perhaps even codependent, tinkering. It was inspired by a chicken salad I first encountered at a sandwich shop on Miami Beach called Stefano's: cubes of chicken breast, celery, and raisins in a spiced mayonnaise. I was also influenced by a chicken salad in Asheville, North Carolina. This one had slivered almonds rather than celery, fried vermicelli noodles, and mandarin oranges. The chicken, though still white meat, had at least been grilled.

I was determined to come up with a chicken salad that would gratify a fuller range of the mouth's largely unspoken desires. So I began to add ingredients, incrementally, in accordance with a very simple standard. As Brecht put it: *"What work does it do?"* (He was talking about words, but the same principle applies to ingredients.)

Thus, the work of the crushed cashews: a crunch for the teeth, a subtle, nutty flavor for the tongue, a burst of fat for both. I added raisins because I wanted something chewy in the mix that would balance the sodium bomb of the cashews. I found brown raisins to have a slight acrid aftertaste, though, so I went with the less acidic golden variety. McIntosh apples provided a crunch that was simultaneously sweet and tart. Celery was my ultimate multitasker: a flavor enhancer, a fibrous element, and a crucial source of moisture.

What enchanted me about this recipe was the chance to experience so many flavors and textures simultaneously, to pivot, in a single bite, from sweet to tangy to salty, from crisp to pillowy soft. (It is for this reason that I chop the chicken and apples finely, so that each bite will contain all five ingredients.)

In my initial recipe, I added a bit of nutmeg, to play off the apples, but refrained from the use of mayonnaise. This was a bit of hubris on my part. I wanted to prove that I could come up with a chicken salad that didn't rely on mayo. But the salad lacked cohesion. It needed a unifying agent, an emulsifier. I tried a few other candidates, with disastrous results. Mustard decimated the subtle flavors. Olive oil proved too, well, oily. Heavy cream was just a very stupid decision.

It was mayo I needed. But I couldn't bring myself to dump a lump of Best Foods onto this symphony. So I decided to dose the stuff up with curry powder. This was six or seven years ago, before curried mayo became something of an haute cuisine cliché.

This decision had something to do, I suspect, with a vague memory of a chicken dish my mother used to prepare, which involved onions, orange juice, and a light dusting of curry powder. "If you can't think of what's missing," she told me once, in relation to this dish, "it's usually curry powder." My immediate concern was that I was going overboard in the flavor department, hot-dogging. In fact, the curried mayo was precisely what the recipe needed, something homely yet exotic, sturdy yet aromatic.

Let me add a final note about cooking as a broader endeavor. Please remember that it is an act of creativity, not of penance. Which is to say, the best recipes I know of require nothing more than two basic acts:

Act One:
The acquisition of good, fresh ingredients

Act Two:
Getting out of the way

With this in mind, I give you . . .

RECIPE

Steve's Ultimate Maple Crunch Chicken Salad

INGREDIENTS:

2 cups smoked chicken (diced straight from the grill)
1 ½ cups McIntosh apples, diced
1 cup celery, thinly sliced
1 cup roasted cashew halves
¾ cup golden raisins
½ cup mayo (more or less to taste)
1 teaspoon curry powder

Dump ingredients in a large bowl.
Mix.

SUGGESTED SERVING:

Straight out of the bowl, with a large wooden spoon.

Eating Fish Alone

Eating fish is something I generally do alone. I eat fish at home only when I am by myself in the house, because of the strong smell. I am alone with sardines on white bread with mayonnaise and lettuce, I am alone with smoked salmon on buttered rye bread, or tuna fish and anchovies in a *salade niçoise*, or a canned salmon salad sandwich, or sometimes salmon cakes sautéed in butter.

I usually order fish when I eat out. I order it because I like it and because it is not meat, which I rarely eat, or pasta, which is usually too rich, or a vegetarian dish, which I am likely to know all too well. I bring a book with me, though often the light over the table is not very good for reading and I am too distracted to read. I try to choose a table with good light, then I order a glass of wine and take out my book. I always want my glass of wine immediately, and I am very impatient until it comes. When it comes, and I have taken my first sip, I put my book down beside my plate and consider the menu. My plan is always to order fish.

I love fish, but many fish should not be eaten anymore, and it has become difficult to know which fish I can eat. I carry with me in my wallet a little folding list put out by the Audubon Society that advises which fish to avoid, which fish to eat with caution, and which fish to eat freely. When I eat with other people I do not take this list out of my wallet, because it is not much fun to have dinner with someone who takes a list like this out of her wallet before she orders. I simply manage without it, though usually I can remember only that I should not eat farmed salmon, or wild salmon, except for wild Alaskan salmon, which is never on the menu.

But when I am alone, I take out my list. No one will imagine, from a nearby table, that this list is what I am looking at. The trouble is, most kinds of fish on restaurant menus are not fish one can eat freely. Some fish one cannot eat at all, ever, and other fish one may eat only if they come from the right place or are caught in the right way. I don't try to ask the waitress how the fish is caught, but I often ask where the fish is from. She usually does not know. This means that no one else has asked her that evening—either no one else is interested, or some are not interested and others know the answer already. If the waitress does not know the answer, she goes away to ask the chef, and then comes back with an answer, though it is usually not the one that I was hoping to hear.

I once asked a completely pointless question about halibut. I did not realize how pointless it was until the waitress had gone off to ask the chef. Pacific halibut is fine to eat, while Atlantic halibut is not. Even though I live on the Atlantic coast, or near it, I asked her where the halibut was from, as though I had forgotten how far away the Pacific Ocean was, or as though halibut would be shipped all the way from the Pacific coast to the Atlantic just for reasons of health or good fishing practices. As it happened, the restaurant was busy and she forgot to ask the chef, and by the time she returned I had realized that I should not order the halibut and was ready to order scallops instead. Scallops, my list said, were neither to be avoided nor to be eaten freely, but to be eaten with caution. I did not know what caution might mean in a restaurant situation, except perhaps that one should ask the waitress and the chef a few more questions than usual. But since even simple questions often do not produce very good answers, I do not expect good answers to detailed questions. Besides, I knew that the waitress and the chef did not have time for detailed questions. Certainly, if scallops were offered on the menu, the waitress or chef would not tell me they were endangered or unclean and advise me not to eat them. I ordered and ate them, and they were good, though I was a little uncomfortable, wondering whether they had been collected in the wrong way or contained toxic substances.

When I eat alone, I have no one to talk to and nothing to do but eat and drink, so my bites of food and my sips of wine are a little too deliberate. I keep thinking, "It's time to take another bite," or "Slow down, the food is almost gone, the meal will be over too soon." I try to read my book in order to make some time go by before I take another bite or another sip. But I can hardly understand what is on the page because I am reading so little at a time. I am also distracted by the other people in the room. I like to watch the waiters and waitresses and other customers very closely, even if they are not very interesting.

The fish on the restaurant menu is often not on my list. Turbot in champagne sauce was offered one night at a very good French restaurant near where I live, but turbot was not on my list. I might have had it, but I was told by the waiter that it was a very mild fish, so I thought it was probably not very tasty. Also, it came with a cheese crust on it. I said I thought the crust would be too rich. The waiter said it was a very thin crust. Even so, I decided against it. There were other fish on the menu: red snapper, which my list instructed me to avoid; Atlantic cod, which is endangered; and salmon, but not wild Alaskan salmon. I gave up on fish and ordered the restaurant's special plate of assorted vegetables, which arrived with small portions of many different vegetables, including fennel bulbs, arranged clockwise around a beautiful golden-brown molded potato cake. The different flavors of the vegetables were unexpectedly exciting, even though so many of them were root vegetables—not only carrots and potatoes but also sautéed radishes, turnips, and parsnips.

The restaurant was owned by a couple from France. The wife greeted the guests and oversaw the service, and the husband cooked. As I left the restaurant that night, on my way to the parking lot I passed the windows of the kitchen. It was brightly lit and I stopped to look in. The chef was alone. He was dressed in white, wearing his chef's cap, and he was slim and active, bending over his chopping block. As far as I could see from that distance, his features were finely modeled, delicate, and intense. As I watched, he tipped his head back slightly and tossed a bit of food into his mouth, pausing to savor it. A younger man came in from my left carrying a tray of something, put it down, and went out again. He did not appear to have anything to do with the cooking. The chef was alone again. I had never before seen a real chef at work, and had never imagined that a chef would work alone in his kitchen. I could have watched him for a long time, but I felt it would be indiscreet to stay, and I walked away.

The last time I ate by myself, I was in a restaurant I chose because there was no alternative. I was far out in the country and it was the only one open. I thought it would not be very good. It had a loud, popular bar in the front. I ordered a beer

this time, and looked at the menu. The fish special was marlin. I tried to think what a marlin was. I had not thought of a
marlin for a long time. Then I pictured a fish sailing through
the air with a large fin on its back, and I was almost sure it
was popular for sport fishing, but I could not imagine what it
tasted like. It was not on my list, but I ordered it anyway. Since
I did not know whether I should avoid it, there was a chance
that it was all right. Even if it wasn't all right, of course, I could
still occasionally have a fish that I should not have.

When she brought the fish, the waitress passed along a message from the chef: he would be waiting to know how I liked
it; it was such a beautiful steak, he said. I was impressed by his
enthusiasm, and as I ate, I paid more careful attention than
usual. The chef had time to be interested in this marlin steak,
I suppose, because it was a Monday night and only one other
table was occupied, in the large dining room, though as I ate
my meal, a few more people came in. Even the bar had only two
customers, small old men in plaid flannel shirts. But with the
loud television and the laughter of the barmaid, who was also
the hostess and the wife of the chef, the bar was still noisy.

The marlin was good, if a little chewy. When the waitress
came by to see how I liked it, I did not tell her it was chewy. I
told her it was very good, and that I liked the delicacy of the
herbs in the sauce. At one point in the meal, as I continued eating slowly, this time without reading, the chef emerged from
the kitchen in the distance. He was a tall man with a slight
stoop to his shoulders. He walked over to the bar to have a

drink and say a few words to his wife and the old men, and then walked back. Before he pushed through the swinging door, he turned a moment to look across the dining room in my direction, curious, I'm sure, to know who was eating his beautiful marlin steak. I looked back at him. I would have waved, but before I thought of it he disappeared through the door.

The serving of food on my plate, the marlin steak and baked potato and vegetable, was generous, and I could not eat all of it. I ate all the vegetables, at least, tender slices of lightly sautéed zucchini with thin strips of red pepper and herbs, and asked the waitress if she would wrap up the rest for me to take home. She was worried; I had eaten only half the fish. "But you did like it?" she asked. She was young. I thought she was the daughter of the chef and the barmaid. I assured her I had. Now I was worried; the chef might not believe I had truly liked the fish, though I had. There was nothing more I could say about it, but, as I paid my bill, I told the waitress I had loved the vegetables. "Most people don't eat them," she said, matter-of-factly. I thought of the waste, and the care with which the chef prepared, over and over again, the vegetables that no one would eat. At least I had eaten his vegetables, and he would know that I had liked them. But I was sorry I had not eaten all of his marlin. I could have done that.

RECIPE

Sardine Sandwich

serves 1

INGREDIENTS:

1 large slice frozen whole-grain bread
1 scallion
3 eggs
$\frac{1}{3}$–$\frac{1}{2}$ can sardines, drained
4 kalamata olives, pitted
2 tablespoons mayonnaise
$\frac{1}{4}$–$\frac{1}{2}$ teaspoon mustard
fresh lemon juice
6–7 prewashed baby romaine leaves

Take the slice of frozen whole-grain bread (it is frozen because you don't use it up fast enough to keep it fresh) and put it in the toaster. (If you are a big eater, use 2 slices for this sandwich and double all quantities.)

Take 1 scallion from your oldest bunch (there are three bunches in your vegetable drawer because you keep buying more, forgetting you already have some; always use up your oldest food first). Peel away the bad parts and you will have the right quantity for the sandwich. Slice it.

Cover the 3 eggs with cold water and put them on to boil. You won't need hard-boiled eggs for this sandwich, but you'll want one for tomorrow's lunch, *salade niçoise*, which is what you really would have preferred for lunch today. You need to boil 3 eggs because two of them will crack in the water and get watery and mushy. You won't throw them out, but you want at least one perfect hard-boiled egg.

Open the can of sardines. (At this point the dog is going to get interested, since you usually give him the "tuna juice" when you open a can of tuna. There is no "sardine juice," just thick oil that wouldn't be good for him, so he's going to be disappointed.) You may get indigestion now, just smelling the sardines. If so, you'll be saved the trouble of making the sandwich—just skip lunch and go off and sit with your indigestion. If not, proceed.

Slice the kalamata olives into thin rounds. (It's hard to remember how long they've been in the fridge, and no one will ever tell you how long you can keep olives safely, but they look all right.) The olives will add interest to the sandwich. (There goes the shell on one of the eggs.)

The bread should be ready now—not toasted, but warm and softened. Cut in half and squirt about 1 tablespoon of mayonnaise on each half. (When your son leaves for college, you should stop buying squeeze bottles of commercial mayonnaise and start making your own with part olive oil and part corn oil.)

With your forefinger, scoop a little mustard out of the jar that is always nearly empty but never quite runs out, thus always annoying you. Scrape this from your finger with a knife and spread on one half of the bread.

Crush and spread a few sardines on the other half of bread in a layer ¼ to ½ inch thick. Cover with sliced olives and scallions. Squeeze fresh lemon juice over the sardines, to taste.

The eggs are finished now. (Only one cracked this time.) Run cold water over them. Change your mind and decide to include one in the sandwich. Peel and slice—it will be a little messy. Distribute in a layer over the sardines. Cover with baby romaine lettuce leaves and the other half of the bread.

Put the rest of the sardines away in a covered container. Relent and let the dog lick the bowl into which you had pointlessly drained sardine oil. (He will be very pleased, and will have a good drink of water afterward.)

The sandwich will be messy, so don't let go of it once you are holding it, and don't try to read any book you value while you eat. If you want a less messy sandwich, try using two larger pieces of softer bread, and put less filling in the sandwich. Will probably still be messy.

Notes from the Nauseous

CARLA SPARTOS

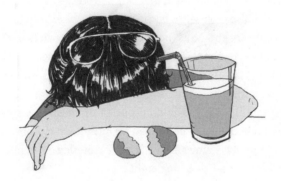

And what if the worst is true? What if there is no God and you only go around once and that's it? Don't you want to be part of the experience? You know, what the hell—it's not all a drag.
— MICKEY SACHS, *Hannah and Her Sisters*

That's the first sane remark I've heard today. Come along, Dexter. I know a formula that's said to pop the pennies off the eyelids of dead Irishmen. — UNCLE WILLIE, *The Philadelphia Story*

Drinking emboldens me. The world is imbued with sparkling possibility by my second lager, screwdriver, or champagne (when it comes to drinking I'm a pragmatist, although I do envy the passions of scotch-and-soda men). This is the first omen, this arrogant nature revealed. It is when I force you to do an iced vodka shot with me because, well, I'm buying. *Here's to friends and friends we'll be, and if perchance we disagree, then fuck you, and here's to me!*

This is also precisely when the Age of Alcohol Enlightenment (alternatively known as the Period of Pronunciation, the Epoch of Addition, or simply, the Ability to Zip One's Jacket) goes into drastic decline. It is how I find myself in a Hell's Kitchen dive at 4 AM with two strippers and a transsexual named Amanda, carousing like old war buddies; or at an illegal after-hours in the Garment District populated by intimidating mobsters and thin-skinned cocaine addicts. We are a motley crew, my fellow champions of self-loathing and I.

But soon those twilight hours are pierced by sunlight: the memories only vaguely intuited and even then accompanied by a grimace. (If I can recount these evenings now, it's because, like Shakespeare's tragedies, they've been enacted a thousand times. And the witnesses, the cursed witnesses! I forced you to do a shot with me so that you too would dwell amidst shadows.) Slowly it burns a hole, this glaring hangover: nausea, headache, dehydration, diarrhea—a litany of questions, which, if I could only answer them correctly, would rid me of this clawing anxiety.

But that's puke in a parfait glass I'm serving you. Don't you think the monk who whips himself does so with a certain satisfaction? Am I to high-five Dostoyevsky's Underground Man when he tells me, "The pleasure came precisely from being too clearly aware of your own degradation; from the feeling of having gone to the uttermost limits"? Got that straight, brother! We thinking men *have* lost all self-respect! We've sunk so low we've come to think highly of our lowness! Why else would I brag so? *Look at me! I hang out with strippers and transsexuals in Hell's Kitchen!*

I want to be at the spotlight's center. Which is precisely why I don't go home after that second drink, while things are still sparkling. Why would I walk off the set right before my big line? Like Antoine Roquentin, Sartre's Nauseous Man, "I had imagined that at certain times my life could take on a rare and precious quality." For Roquentin, it was the exotic trips to Rome, Barcelona, Baray Prah-Kan that gave his existence temporary sheen. But nowhere has that radiance been more apparent to me than at the local bar.

But now, in the morning, I suspect that I am painfully dull. Because if the hangover is anything, it is the caster of doubt. What if these adventures of the night have really been anything but? I can no longer remember the meaning of my exploits; they are cold, hard things knocking around in my brain. The debauched parties, the notorious friends, the stories that fill volumes are gone. Once the hangover sets in, I am plagued by the same idea that strikes Roquentin upon unearthing his postcards and pictures of Spain and Spanish Morocco: *the idea that he has had no adventures.* How could these snapshots, these frozen images, give his life any more meaning than they would to a pebble on a beach?

When I no longer believe in the narrative I've woven for myself, I have reached my lowest point. I have just woken up naked in a stranger's bed and all that remains inside me are traces of alien warmth. My reptilian brain, which tracks my fear, wonders: *What has been taken from me?* My human brain, always the last to know, replies: *Where is my pocketbook? How did I get this bruise?*

At this point, I must cling to one certainty: all is fleeting.

I've come to understand that the hangover originates in the very first sip. Like the quinine in my gin and tonic, it circulates the blood, bitter, waiting.

What's done is done, and right now, the only surefire cure for my malaise is to have another drink. I don't care if the mere thought of a gin and tonic makes me gag. My prescription only calls for one.

Eye-openers once fueled civilized society. Our grandparents adored them. And although "eye-opener" can refer to any drink that picks you up, the Eye-Opener is an actual rum-and-egg–based cocktail that, according to David Wondrich, author of *Esquire Drinks*, turned up in the literature sometime in the mid-nineteenth century. Like so many cocktails, it enjoys a rather ambiguous past: Wondrich traces the lineage of the *Esquire* recipe to Frank Newman, a Brit working in Paris who published *American Bar: Recettes des Boissons Anglaises et Americaines.* "Here, loosely translated," according to Wondrich, "is the eye-opener from Newman's third edition (1907). Put some cracked ice in a silver cup; [add] one coffee-spoon powdered sugar, three dashes curaçao, two dashes absinthe, four dashes crème de noyau, one egg yolk, [and] one liqueur-glass rum. Shake, strain, and serve."

The Eye-Opener may also contain apricot brandy, grenadine, orange curaçao, crème de cacao, anisette, pastis, and yes, if you're feeling particularly vicious, absinthe. Its medicinal taste, like licorice eggnog or a peptic Pynchonian confection (cherry-quinine petit four? eucalyptus-flavored fondant?), isn't half-bad, and the raw egg has the added effect of making you feel like a boxer the morning of a big bout.

It is an elixir that achieves what two Tylenols and a gallon of water can't. Coffee pales in comparison! A Big Mac is powerless in its presence! Stand on your head and Om to Allah and still you will feel like death incarnate, but have an Eye-Opener and observe the color return to your cheeks. *I'm such a dodo!* you will exclaim. *I kicked my purse under the bed after I tripped and fell on it. Then I passed out cold!*

But good luck finding somebody who can whip one up: A bartender at that bastion of bluebloods, Bemelmans Bar at the Carlyle Hotel, told me no one has ordered one in thirty years easy. "I used to make it when I was a kid," he said. "I think it has an egg in it." Which seems strange, considering that excess and the cocktail are as American as a blitzed G. Dubya careening down a Texas highway; as a nation we've invented a whole host of remedies for eating and drinking too much. So why is the Eye-Opener considered so horribly old-fashioned? And how did abstinence become a virtue to a people who spawned the slogan "I can't believe I ate the whole thing"?

The Eye-Opener has gotten an unjustifiably bad rap. It is not going to make your hangover worse; it is not merely prolonging the inevitable. No, an Eye-Opener does only what it purports, which is why it belongs to that delightful family of drinks known as "restorative cocktails." But still the Eye-Opener retains its undeserved reputation as the preferred poison of the jowled letch. The CAGE Questionnaire, which diagnoses alcoholism, asks, "Have you ever had a drink first thing in the morning or to get rid of a hangover (Eye-Opener)?" These researchers obviously haven't watched any Cary Grant movies lately or they wouldn't spoil our Sunday brunches with such presumptuous questions.

Overindulgence used to be a weakness akin to chasing skirts or telling dirty jokes; it signified fast and loose morals, not a diseased mind. In *The Philadelphia Story*, Cary Grant plays a recovering alcoholic with a knack for mixing drinks. But it strikes none of the revelers who ring around this suave creature to deny him a cocktail shaker. It's not that the partygoers don't recognize alcoholism (in the films of this period, someone always has a bulbous-nosed brother, uncle, cousin, or pal with a penchant for drink—in this case the affable but slurring Uncle Willie), but they're certainly not wagging fingers. When everybody wakes up with wicked hangovers—including a peaked Katherine Hepburn on the morning of her wedding day—Grant takes swift action by suggesting to Uncle Willie they find "Eye-Openers" in the pantry.

Drinking's a continuum, not some line that's irreparably crossed with a single AM swill. Unlike the ritualized Bloody Mary, the Eye-Opener is an "in case of emergency, break glass" tonic reserved for women about to marry the wrong men—or with fathers just found guilty of treason. In Alfred Hitchcock's *Notorious*, Grant serves an Eye-Opener to Ingrid Bergman, with whom he shared a bottle the previous evening. Bergman wakes up spinning—brilliantly conveyed by Hitchcock's rotating camera—to find a cloudy drink perched on her nightstand. "Go on, drink it," says Grant.

Which is the first sane remark *I've* heard all day. So I mix myself an Eye-Opener, and since I'm a glutton for punishment, I'll throw in a splash of absinthe, so popular with the existentialists from whom I inherited my nauseous lot. (If you're lacking the hallucinatory liqueur, pastis will make a fine substitute; it shares the same herbal anise taste minus the illegal wormwood.) I measure in the obligatory rum and yolk and liqueurs gathering dust on my bar and agitate all to a calm, pale yellow froth. And drink. Fuck it.

RECIPE

My Eye-Opener

INGREDIENTS:

1 shot light rum
1 teaspoon absinthe
1 teaspoon orange curaçao
1 teaspoon white crème de cacao
½ teaspoon superfine sugar
1 egg yolk
Several ice cubes

Combine and shake enthusiastically.
Strain into a glass. Serve.

Dinner with the Borgias

POWER, POLITICS, PASSION, PROVENDER, AND
POISON IN THE ITALIAN RENAISSANCE

LISA GROSSMAN

Cardinal Spada knew what these invitations meant; since Christianity, so eminently civilizing, had made progress in Rome, it was no longer a centurion who came from the tyrant with a message, "Caesar wills that you die," but a legate a latere, who came with a smile on his lips to say from the pope, "His Holiness requests you to dine with him."

—ALEXANDRE DUMAS, *The Count of Monte Cristo*

The year is 1497; the place, a vineyard near Sampierdarena. You are a newly created cardinal, guest of honor at the table of His Holiness Pope Alexander VI.

Will you get home alive?

It was too late, for he had already drunk a glass of excellent wine. . . . An hour afterwards a physician declared he was poisoned through eating mushrooms.

—Dumas, *The Count of Monte Cristo*

Probably not.

And the whisper will go round in the streets of Rome that the Borgias—"that diabolical trio . . . that mocking parody of the heavenly trinity"—have added another to their long list of poisoning victims. That, after all, is a cornerstone of the Borgia legend: poison, treachery, and incest, not necessarily in that order. By and large, modern scholarship acquits them of these charges; but in popular legend, in the eyes of their contemporaries, they are guilty as sin. They *are* guilt, personified.

It's been five busy years since 1492, when Rodrigo Borgia bought his way into the papacy. There's nothing random about his choice of papal name: his ambitions echo those of Alexander the Great, and in styling himself Alexander VI he has deliberately suited the cognomen to the intent. The Church, for him, is less a vocation than a path to unprecedented secular power. In the interests of consolidating this power, he has put his offspring to good use: Cesare is a cardinal; Giovanni commander of the papal army; Lucrezia married to a cousin of the powerful Duke of Milan; Goffredo—well, never mind Goffredo.

There's more important game afoot.

Alexander is fighting to gain control of Romagna, and it's getting to be rather an expensive proposition even for his deep pockets. Cesare, whose talents and inclinations have always been military rather than ecclesiastical, is fiercely jealous of his brother Giovanni, who by all accounts is not much of a campaigner. France, the perpetual enemy of Rome, has given up trying to annex Naples and has made peace with Milan, and this effectively turns Rome's strategic perspective on its head: suddenly Milan becomes the enemy, Naples the desirable ally.

Cesare's problem is solved when Giovanni is found floating facedown in the Tiber, a dagger in his throat. Inheriting his brother's responsibilities and most of his titles, Cesare happily gives up the Church and sets about solving his father's problems in Romagna. Papa, meanwhile, has been selling indulgences and birettas in all directions to build up his war chest. As for Milan and Naples, the solution is simple: he has but to annul Lucrezia's marriage to the Milanese Giovanni Sforza and marry her off instead to Alfonso of Aragon, grandson of the king of Naples.

Sforza, however, refuses to cooperate. Despite all papal persuasion, after five years of marriage he is curiously reluctant to declare himself impotent. But impotent he is—politically if not sexually, the Vatican being too powerful a foe to resist. So Lucrezia, though several months pregnant, is declared *virgo intacta*; the marriage is annulled; and Sforza turns his energies to spreading rumors.

Things get nasty. And complicated.

~~~~~~~~~~~~~~~~~~~~~~~~~~~~~

Dare to be true: nothing can need a ly;
A fault, which needs it most, grows two thereby.
—George Herbert, *The Church-Porch*

From a warp of incest and a woof of poison, Sforza weaves an intricate web of whole cloth and cuts it to fit the Borgias. He lets it be known that Alexander can have only one motive for demanding Lucrezia's freedom: he wants her for himself. Of course, as Sforza then hastens to add, the pope will still have to compete with his sons for the favors of his daughter. With the two remaining sons, that is—Sforza now attributes Giovanni Borgia's murder to Cesare Borgia's "trademark" poison dagger, the motive again being jealousy over Lucrezia. The fratricide, he then insinuates, is not Cesare's first expedient use of poison: not only is it well-known that Cesare and his holy father murdered the unfortunate Turkish hostage Prince D'Jem by means of a farewell supper in 1495, it now appears that, hoping to save themselves the trouble of pursuing the divorce, they recently attempted to poison Giovanni Sforza himself.

Lucrezia's ex-husband brings a certain amount of authority to his subject. Poisoning, as one contemporary remarked, has long been "part of the manners and custom of Italy," and no one knows more about it than the Sforzas. It is generally understood that the late Duke of Milan, Gian Galeazzo Sforza, was poisoned by his uncle Lodovico ("Il Moro") in 1494 for no less a prize than the duchy of Milan itself; Gian Galeazzo's half-sister Caterina Sforza will claim credit in her memoirs for devising the *veleno a termine*, an insidious toxin that may well be the first time-release formula in history. Giovanni Sforza, second cousin to the murdered duke, does not scruple to lay this and other such lethal inventions at the Borgia door.

The Borgias' poisoning ways can be traced back, it is hinted, to an elaborate attempt on the life of the antipope Benedict XIII in 1418—though the Borgia connection is tenuous at best. It seems Benedict was fond of sweets, so he was given arsenic in two forms: the standard white powder, combined with egg and sugar to make a coating for his favorite sugar biscuits; and the red-orange disulphide *realgar*, concealed in candied citron.

Despite a hefty dose, Benedict survived—which suggests that perhaps successful poisonings were not as prevalent as many people feared. Nevertheless, most important families, wisely choosing safe over sorry, employed tasters—even at the heavy cost of eating all their dinners cold.

Outside of the antipope affair, little is really known about the methods used by the legendary poisoners of the Borgia stripe. Much is conjectured, however, and the conjectures tend to contradict each other, almost to the point of canceling each other out.

There was *La Cantarella*, attributed variously to the Sforzas and the Borgias; some aver that it killed instantly, some that it took hours or even days to manifest itself, some that it could do either, according to the requirements of the poisoner in each individual case. *La Cantarella* is described variously as a fine white powder, slightly sweet, and as a flavorless liquid; judging from accounts of the victims' symptoms it is probably based on some form of arsenic, possibly combined with phosphorus, though there are also suggestions that it may take its name and properties from cantharides. It took other names from its larger purpose: it was sometimes fancifully referred to as "Powder of Inheritance," "Elixir of Succession," or, more poetically, "Eternity Powder."

Arsenic seems to have been the general favorite, but two-and-twenty substances in all were known to be poisonous, and all were fair game. Sometimes these would appear in combination with arsenic; Leonardo, for instance, once offered to create weapons for the Duke of Milan, including a poison gas made from "lime, sulphide of arsenic, and verdigris."

Herbal poisons were also handy. In some stories Lucrezia is supposed to have killed inconvenient lovers with the contents of a poison ring stirred into their wine; the most likely candidate for this would have been powdered foxglove, a crude form of digitalis.

Another popular if controversial choice: pulverized diamonds, which could be sprinkled on food, mixed into potions, or simply administered "straight" by the spoonful. Controversial because many doctors believed that jewels had mystical healing properties; in 1534 Pope Clement VII proved them very much mistaken by dying of his prescribed treatment: fourteen tablespoons of pulverized gems. Long before that, however, ground diamonds were being used for their lethal powers. Lodovico "Il Moro" is supposed to have arranged such a death for Lorenzo de' Medici; the Turkish Sultan Bajazet (elder brother—and murderer by proxy—of the unfortunate D'Jem) met a similar end at the hands of his son; ground diamonds were also a famous part of Catherine de' Medici's arsenal. Benvenuto Cellini would have been another ground-diamond victim, but that a thieving lapidary supplied his would-be murderer with ground beryl instead.

Poisons, of course, were not always ingested with food. Catherine de' Medici and her "personal perfumer" (for which read personal poisoner, alchemist, kabbalist, and generally shady character) elevated this uneaten style to an art, offering perfumed gloves to one victim, a beautifully bound book to another. The perfume, of course, was deadly once inhaled. The book was harmless enough but for certain pages that stuck together; the unsuspecting reader would lick his finger, turn the page, lick again, turn again . . . and die within the chapter. Catherine was also fond of the old henbane-in-the-ear trick, which she may have learned from the murder of the Duke of Urbino in 1538—a story also well-known to one William Shakespeare.

Caterina Sforza, a termagant who fought valiantly against the Borgias for several years, distinguished herself in the poisoning arena with a particularly diabolical attempt on the life of Alexander VI himself. In 1499 she wrote a letter to him, and before sending it she arranged to have it contaminated by a deadly infectious disease, which was then running rampant in her province of Forlì. (Would this have worked, if her messengers hadn't been intercepted? Expert opinion is divided.)

And speaking of His Holiness . . . he and Cesare are supposed to have had a couple of other poisonous tricks, possibly involving distilled snake venom, up their sleeves.

~~~~~~~~~~~~~~~~~~~~~~~~~~~~~

The poisoned key . . . lay always on the pope's mantelpiece, so that when His Holiness wished to destroy some one of his intimates, he bade him open a certain cupboard: on the handle of the key there was a little spike, and as the lock of the cupboard turned stiffly the hand would naturally press, the lock would yield, and nothing would have come of it but a trifling scratch: the scratch was mortal. Cesare wore a ring made like two lions' heads, and . . . he would turn the stone on the inside when he was shaking hands with a friend. Then the lions' teeth became the teeth of a viper, and the friend died cursing Borgia.

—Dumas, *Crimes of the Borgias*

~~~~~~~~~~~~~~~~~~~~~~~~~~~~~

In 1498, while Giovanni Sforza is industriously spreading his own brand of poison, his former wife Lucrezia obediently furthers her father's political agenda by marrying Alfonso of Aragon (who ironically happens to be Sforza's second cousin). Against all odds the two eighteen-year-olds actually fall in love. With each other.

Of course, such a bizarre state of affairs cannot last very long. Shortly after the marriage, the political pendulum swings again; relations between Naples and the Vatican begin to deteriorate. Cesare and Alexander now cast a covetous eye on the rich Este family, the rulers of Ferrara, who in wistful hindsight appear far more desirable as in-laws.

July 1500. Cesare sends a band of masked toughs to attack Alfonso of Aragon on the steps of St. Peter's. Alfonso is gravely wounded; Lucrezia is determined to save his life. She nurses him devotedly and vigilantly, cooking all his food herself for fear of poisoning. He nearly recovers. One day, however, Cesare dupes her into leaving the sickroom for a few minutes; when she returns Alfonso is dead. Cesare, who has been heard to mutter that what failed at lunch will be successful at supper, openly admits to the murder but justifies it as self-defense.

"Trademark" poison dagger? Strangulation? No one is sure.

Rumors fly. Giovanni Sforza's scandals have taken on considerable momentum, fueled by tales of orgies at the Vatican, by open speculation about Lucrezia's love life, and most recently by suspicions about the nature of Lucrezia's nursing and its bearing on her husband's death. Lucrezia is widely perceived as an incestuous harlot and a black widow—mad, bad, and dangerous to marry. Nowhere does all this innuendo cause more concern than in the ducal house of Ferrara; Lucrezia's prospective groom, Alfonso d'Este, being first cousin to the recently departed Alfonso of Aragon. All in all, the Este family is exceedingly reluctant to risk the alliance.

It's the substantial dowry that finally wins them over. In 1501 the wedding is celebrated with all due pomp (including the first appearance of tagliatelle, created in tribute to the bride's long golden hair), and Lucrezia at twenty-two becomes Duchess of Ferrara. It's an auspicious occasion for her, the beginning of a new and altogether more serene life. She will prove herself an able administrator and a gracious patron of the arts, will gradually gain the love and respect of the Ferrarese, and will never again be a political pawn for her father and brother.

And all this thanks to the dowry provided by her father, largely the fruit of his last hurrah of coffer-filling.

〰〰〰〰〰〰〰〰〰〰〰〰〰

Oh, let us never, never doubt
What nobody is sure about!

—Hilaire Belloc, *The Microbe*

〰〰〰〰〰〰〰〰〰〰〰〰〰

In the five centuries since his death, the final four years of Alexander's papacy (1500–1503) have been a favorite topic of historians, novelists, and everything in between. Much of the infamy attached to the Borgia name can be traced to the sensationalist writers of the nineteenth century, who well knew that the really lurid stories make the best copy. Balzac, Hugo, and Dumas gleefully seized on the most outrageous charges of antipapist writers like Tommasi and Infessura (charges which in turn were largely based on the vengeful allegations of Giovanni Sforza et al.), embroidering heavily and presenting the results to a gullible public as simple fact.

Dumas was perhaps the most shameless of the bunch, a fine two-fisted writer who never let the facts get in the way of a good story. Same technique for the histories as for the novels: take equal parts juicy innuendo and outright fabrication, combine into one steaming dish of iniquity, season with high melodrama, and serve forth. The evidence doesn't support his versions, but they're great stuff, far more gripping than the actual events; they are also far more widely believed, so much so as to constitute a kind of secular apocrypha. And which, after all, is the more true—which influences history more—fact or popular belief? *Se non è vero, è ben trovato.*

Herewith, then—all swashes buckled—Alexander's final fund-raiser.

By 1500 corpses were turning up rather frequently in the Tiber—and elsewhere. The husband of Cesare's latest mistress; a bishop from Portugal, suspected of spying for France; Cesare's various discarded lovers, male or female, willing or unwilling—all neatly disposed of. It was His Holiness the Pope, however, who introduced the profit angle.

When the lords of Sermoneta died (one by strangulation, the other by poison) conveniently intestate, the pope inherited their lands. But the death of Archbishop Agnelli of Cosenza raised the ante: his poisoning left not only considerable personal property but also several ecclesiastical offices to be disposed of—through simony, of course. Dumas brazenly claims that Alexander VI now created the Law of Property Ecclesiastical (which had actually been in effect for some four hundred years), whereby priests and cardinals were deprived of the right to will their property to anyone but the Church. His Holiness then set about cherry-picking targets, simply poisoning the richest remaining cardinal whenever he found himself a little short of the ready.

In 1503 he went himself one better, creating nine new cardinals for fun and profit. It was a beautiful plan.

First, the cardinals elected would leave all their offices vacant; these offices would fall into the hands of the pope, and he would sell them; Second, each of them would buy his election, for 40,000 ducats; Finally, since as cardinals they would by law lose the right of making a will, the pope, in order to inherit from them, had only to poison them: this put him in the position of a butcher who, if he needs money, has only to cut the throat of the fattest sheep in the flock.

—Dumas, *Crimes of the Borgias*

In the pope's vineyard at Sampierdarena, the table was laid for the celebration of the new cardinals' nomination. "But," Dumas continues, "it seemed as though God wished to show His strange vicar on earth that He was angered by the mockery of sacred things." The poison, on this occasion, was in specially prepared bottles of wine—and despite all best-laid plans the bottles were accidentally switched. In the crowning irony of the Borgia papacy, Alexander and Cesare drank the draught intended for their fattest sheep.

They shook, they stared as white's their shirt:
Them it was their poison hurt.

—A. E. Housman, *Terence, This Is Stupid Stuff*

Alexander VI died two weeks later. Cesare survived, but quickly and prudently sank into obscurity; a sad comedown for the man who first dreamed of uniting Italy, the man of whom Macchiavelli was to write, "Cesare Borgia is the prince who best knows how to make and unmake men according to their desserts."

UNWHOLESOME FARE

Which poison was which? Were *La Cantarella* and the *veleno a termine* actually one and the same? It's been suggested, and anything is possible. The range of symptoms attributed to them, jointly and severally, is certainly broad enough. The recipe for the *veleno a termine* does exist, but it is written in code, which is no doubt just as well. Here, however, are two approaches to *La Cantarella*; they are not recommended for home use.

A strong dose of arsenic was administered to a bear; as soon as the poison began to take effect, he was hung up by his heels; convulsions supervened, and a froth deadly and abundant ran out from his jaws; it was this froth, collected into a silver vessel and transferred into a bottle hermetically sealed, that made the liquid poison.

—Dumas, *Crimes of the Borgias*

According to one report the raw material of the "cantar-ella," or its original crude form, was obtained in this man-ner. Some animal, by preference a pig, was slaughtered and disemboweled. The entrails were then freely sprin-kled with pure arsenic. The poison checked but did not entirely arrest the ensuing process of putrefaction. After allowing a certain time to elapse, the semi-putrid matter was squeezed out. The juice thus obtained became far more deadly than arsenic in its pure form but continued just as tasteless.

—John Bond, *In the Pillory*

It might be argued that to invite someone to a dinner at which he is to be poisoned is in itself the ultimate lie; to serve him food that is merely unwholesome may be almost equally dishonest. Nutrition being a less than exact science during the sixteenth century, doctors tended to distrust certain foods simply because they didn't under-stand them; chief among these was cheese, with eels and crustaceans a close second. So recipes using any of these "dangerous" ingredients usually carried a kind of surgeon-general's disclaimer.

Bartolomeo Sacchi *detto* Platina wrote of his White Pie: "This is very nourishing, slow to be digested; it warms the liver, brings on obstructions and causes stones and is bad for the eyes and nerves." The next recipe, also a pie, ends: "This is even worse than the one above." His sweet Lenten crawfish pie comes with the admonition: "This dish harms all parts of the body." And one of his eel pie recipes has this to recommend it: "When finally cooked, serve it to your enemies, for it has nothing good in it."

Could literal poison be much worse?

The Lotus-Eaters

JEFF KOEHLER

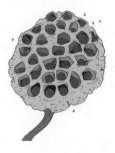

E arly in their voyage from Troy, Odysseus and his band of sailors tossed about on a stormy sea for nine days, reaching, on the tenth, the land of the Lotophagi, the Lotus-eaters. After the crew had eaten and drunk water, three men went ashore:

> They started at once, and went about among the Lotus-eaters, who did them no hurt, but gave them to eat of the lotus, which was so delicious that those who ate of it left off caring about home, and did not even want to go back and say what had happened to them, but were for staying and munching lotus with the Lotus-eaters without

thinking further of their return; nevertheless, though they wept bitterly I forced them back to the ships and made them fast under the benches. Then I told the rest to go on board at once, lest any of them should taste of the lotus and leave off wanting to get home, so they took their places and smote the grey sea with their oars.

—Homer, *The Odyssey*, translation by Samuel Butler

This place is clearly one of myth. Many scholars and adventurers, though, believe that Homer based Odysseus's journeys in *The Odyssey* on actual wanderings of Phoenician merchants, and among them the model for Lotusland is generally accepted as being the island of Djerba, off Tunisia's southern coast near Libya.

I spent the first part of the holy month of Ramadan this year on Djerba. From above, at the end of a short flight from Tunis, it initially looked disappointingly prosaic, a brown speck lying off the edge of the Sahara that barely breached the surface of the sea.

Its mythic allure, though, soon began to reveal itself in Houmt Souk, an ancient city built around a series of central souks and painted uniformly white with Wedgwood blue doors and wooden shutters. I arrived as the sun was close to setting and the breaking of the fast approached. Shops were hurriedly taking in their wares, closing up. People hustled past with last-minute purchases of bread and semolina pastries stuffed with dates.

I climbed up to the roof of the converted *funduq* where I was staying. The streets below had emptied. The call to prayer sounded from a nearby minaret, then another, tripping a daisy chain of calls from the minarets that spiked up across the low cityscape. A lengthy prayer—tinny, melodic, passionate—was followed by a thunderous BOOM! and a final series of *Allah o akbar*. Then absolute silence. I smelled cigarette smoke and, some minutes later, heard laughter.

The squarish island, measuring some fifteen miles across, is umbilically tethered to the mainland by a four-mile-long Roman-built causeway. In the past, its position halfway across Africa's Mediterranean crown was of keen geopolitical interest to many great empires; the island was conquered by the Phoenicians, Carthaginians, Romans, Arabs, and French. Modern Djerbans, though, are mostly of Berber origin. (There was once a significant community of Jews who, according to local legend, settled here after fleeing Jerusalem in the mid-sixth century BC.) Especially in rural areas, a number of people still wear unadorned open-necked robes and low, wide-brimmed straw hats, with the women pulling finely embroidered white shawls around them.

While the western coast remains largely inaccessible, the northern and eastern coasts, with their long beaches of fine white sand, have been developed with an eight-mile-long continuum of sprawling resorts. Dispersed inland are numerous vernacular mosques, smooth washed-white structures with flanking buttresses, enclosed courtyards, and thin, tapering minarets shaped like truncated pyramids. Shading these, and giving the dusty isle a bucolic feel, are date palms; trees bearing olives, pomegranates, figs, grenadines, apricots; vineyards of small sweet grapes grown for raisins.

But what, in this place long famed for its fruit, could have been Homer's model for the lotus?

Some say dates, but most often the lotus is identified as the jujube, a round drupe—a fruit with a thin, almost leathery skin, fleshy middle, and hard, bony stone that encases the seed—from various species of tree belonging to the genus *Zizyphus*. Jujubes have been cultivated in China for four thousand years and grow from there intermittently westward to the Mediterranean. The most common is *Z. jujuba*, which (though far from well-known) I can find in my local market in Barcelona from the first days of September into the beginning of November. *Gínjols*, as they are called in Catalan, are the size and shape of walnuts, with delicate ruby-brown skin, brilliant white flesh, and an oval-shaped pit. The taste is rather unremarkable, something between an unripe pear and a date. (A common Catalan expression is *Més trempat que un gínjol*, roughly "Happier than a jujube." While everybody knows the expression here, nobody seems to be able to explain the link between happiness and jujubes.)

Homer, however, would have been referring to the North African species, *Z. lotus*, a thorny shrub that produces small, yellowish-brown fruit about the size of a pea. In Djerba the drupe is called *annab*, a word that, written, looks similar to the Arabic for grape (*anab*, which is pronounced with a much shorter *n* sound). *Annab* grows largely in the central northern and eastern parts of the island, and can be found in Houmt Souk's *marché couvert* during its brief early-autumn season. Fresh, they are eaten out of your hand, tasting similar to a date, though with a large pit there is relatively little of the floury white flesh. As one woman put it, "You don't stop eating them, you can't stop, until the bowl is empty."

The Roman scholar Pliny the Elder was clearly describing *annab* two thousand years ago in his *Natural History* under the heading "Of the tree lotos," worth quoting at some length, here in Philemon Holland's 1601 translation:

> In the same coast of Affrick which regardeth Italie, there groweth Lotos. . . . Many sorts there be of the Lote tree, and those for the most part according to their divers and severall fruits. Howbeit ordinarily the fruit is as big as a Beane, and of yellow colour as Saffron; yet before it is full ripe, it chaungeth into sundry colors, like as grapes doe. It groweth thicke among the branches of the tree, in manner of Myrtle berries, and not like to the Cherries of Italie: and in those plants above named, the meat thereof is so sweet and pleasant, that it hath given the name both to a nation and a countrey, insomuch as the people be called Lotophagi: and withall, so welcome be

all straungers thither, and so well contented with their
entertainment, that they forget their own native soile,
for the love they have to this fruit, when they have once
taken to it.

Herodotus, too, writing five centuries earlier in *The History*,
seems to describe the same:

There is a cape that projects into the sea from the land
of the Gindanes, and there dwell the Lotophagi, who live
solely from the enjoyment of the lotus fruit. The fruit of
the lotus is about as big as a mastic berry and in sweetness is like the fruit of the palm tree. The Lotophagi also
make wine of this fruit.

—*translation by David Grene*

~~~~~~~~~~~~~~~~~~~~~~~~~

Homer didn't call them Lotus-drinkers, but one popular local
beverage was put to me as the original lotus: *lagmi*, made from
the sap of the palm tree. Found year-round, but especially plen-
tiful from April to October, it is drunk fresh or fermented into
potent hooch. (It ferments quickly because of its high sugar
content.) The upper part of the trunk is tapped and the sap is
drained into a *gargoulette*, a conical two-handled clay jug. In
Houmt Souk's market there is usually a farmer sitting with one
of these jugs selling *lagmi*. But, because it was Ramadan, he
wasn't there during my stay. I could only find a rather belliger-

ent man with a bad eye selling old plastic water bottles refilled with cloudy *lagmi*. I bought a 50 ml bottle for about a dollar and took it back to the hotel. ("Today is good, tomorrow makes you crazy," the manager said with a throaty laugh.) The liquid was a smoky opaque color, slightly thicker than water, and smelled of dank yeast. But it was sweet—incredibly sweet—and tasty. (As for commercial distillates, there is one from dates and another from figs called *boukha*, though these only seemed popular as duty-free items among departing German tourists.)

However debatable the exact origins of the lotus, its meaning is indisputable. The concept of a place where one eats a fruit, sinks into a dreamy forgetfulness, and loses all desire to return home was common currency among the Greeks and Romans. (Plato mentions it in *The Republic* as matter-of-factly as we would refer to Las Vegas or Paris.) The idea, though, isn't just stuck in the literature of antiquity, but has remained a timeless motif.

One of the earliest references to the lotus fruit in English is in Edmund Spenser's 1591 poem "Virgil's Gnat" ("And them amongst the wicked Lotos grew, / Wicked, for holding guilefully away / Vllyses men"). A few centuries later the lotus got the full treatment in Alfred Lord Tennyson's languorous poem "The Lotos-Eaters" (1832):

And round about the keel with faces pale,
Dark faces pale against that rosy flame,
The mild-eyed melancholy Lotos-eaters came.

When the mariners eat from "that enchanted stem, / Laden with flower and fruit", they are instantly hooked and cry out, "We will no longer roam." For Tennyson's men the lotus offers a narcotic release from the hard work and obligations back home—here, Victorian England. We don't know if they go native or are able to return. Tennyson simply leaves them in choric song, dreaming of "Eating the Lotos day by day."

In the fifth chapter of James Joyce's *Ulysses*, unofficially titled "Lotus-eaters" by Joyce himself, Bloom wanders (to the post office, church, and pharmacy) and broods on, among other things, Ireland's own two lotus fruits: the Eucharist, with its "Blind faith" that "lulls all pain"; and Guinness porter, which he envisions as "a lazy pooling swirl of liquor bearing along wide-leaved flowers of its froth." Among a bazaar of perfumes, oils, and ointments in the pharmacy, Bloom buys a cake of lemony soap and floats dreamily toward the public bath, imagining himself reclining "in a womb of warmth," his penis like "a languid floating flower."

Occasionally the Lotus-eater imagery post-Joyce is original, rich, and figuratively surprising, as in Ted Hughes's poem "The Afterbirth," from his harrowing and compelling 1998 collection *Birthday Letters*:

Huddled on the floor, the afterbirth
Was already offal.
There was the lotus-eater's whole island
Dragged out by its roots, into the light,

And flopped onto blood-soaked newsprint—a tangled
Puddle of dawn reds and evening purples,
To be rubbished.

Usually, though, Lotus-eaters have but fleeting cameos, lurching in a drugged stupor through works such as John Steinbeck's *Travels with Charley*:

The old port with narrow streets and cobbled surfaces, smoke-grimed, goes into a period of desolation inhabited at night by the vague ruins of men, the lotus eaters who struggle daily towards unconsciousness by way of raw alcohol.

Yet such literary flourish seems especially distant when read on Djerba itself, and the inherent tint of menace too dark for a place bleached with brilliant light. The only work that relates to my own experience on the island of the fabled Lotophagi is Daniel Mason's *The Piano Tuner*. The Kurtz-like Dr. Anthony Carroll, ensconced in a remote British fort in nineteenth-century Burma, is unable to return home: "Perhaps I stay simply because I cannot leave," he says to the piano tuner who has journeyed to this jungle outpost to tune a rare grand piano. At the end of the novel, Carroll tears out the Lotus-eater episode from his copy of *The Odyssey* and scrawls a note to the tuner that reads, simply, "For Edgar Drake, who has tasted."

Indeed, that sentiment was with me on Djerba—though not from any Homeric fruit, rather from the beauty and slow ways of the island, the charm of the Berbers. Perhaps the lotus, as I was told by more than one Djerban, was simply a metaphor for the island itself.

Such allure. From its famous red-tinted fish couscous and those luminous white mosques hidden in groves of stooped olive trees, from evenings in packed *chicha* cafés smoking apple-flavored tobacco, the din of boisterous card players, an Egyptian soap opera roaring on the TV. One morning even the wind seduced. It appeared early, not long after the muezzin's first call to prayer. Crossing my cool room, I could feel a thin layer of grit on the floor, and, opening the door, I was hit with a swirling blast of hot, textured air carrying with it the musty smell of a deeper Africa. Sand had gathered in small drifts in the courtyard of the *funduq* and was, I would see once it got light, filling the horizon, leaving a bald spot of blue sky above. At that moment, in an eddy of Saharan dust, I felt the familiar tug that once relentlessly propelled me around this continent and then Asia for four years.

But home (a young daughter, an expecting wife) pulled harder as I sat over thick slices of warm baguette with butter and fig jam, a hard-boiled egg, and glasses of sweet black tea in a closed breakfast nook, sheltered from the wind and a short, hissing downpour that merely dimpled the shifting sand patches.

As much as the island induces a desire to stay, home is hard to forget and harder to forgo. Such is the Janus face of travel: the pull of the road's pleasures and the pull of home's comforts. The desire to escape and the desire to return. What moves the lotus fruit into the realm of myth is its great promise to fulfill the former while dissolving the latter.

Like most who visit, beginning with Odysseus, I left. But some do stay. Those, Djerbans say, "have taken the lotus."

RECIPE

Sweet Couscous with Dates and Nuts

This sweet couscous, called *masfouf* in Tunisia and Algeria and *seffa* in Morocco, is often eaten during Ramadan once the fast has been broken. Traditionally this recipe calls for the uncooked type of couscous that needs to be triple-steamed in a *couscoussière*. This version uses the more readily available boxed (and presteamed) couscous.

serves 6

INGREDIENTS:

3 ½ cups water
1 ½ ounces unsalted butter

½ teaspoon salt

2 cups couscous

1 ½ cups sugar

½ cup whole almonds

1 cup dates, such as Deglet Noor

½ cup shelled unsalted pistachios

2 teaspoons essence of orange blossom

1 tablespoon ground cinnamon for dusting

1 tablespoon confectioners' sugar for dusting

Bring 2 ½ cups of water, the butter, and the salt to boil in a large saucepan. Remove from heat and pour in couscous in a steady stream. Stir with a fork and cover. Let sit for 15 to 20 minutes.

Prepare syrup. Combine remaining 1 cup water with the sugar in a small saucepan. Bring to a boil and remove from heat, stirring until sugar has dissolved. Set aside.

Slip skins off almonds and gently heat in a frying pan until warm and fragrant.

While these heat, pit the dates and cut into cubes, leaving 4 dates whole for decoration.

Roughly chop half of the almonds in a food processor, leaving the rest whole for decoration. Shell pistachios and grind half, leaving the rest whole for decoration as well.

Fluff couscous with a fork to separate the grains, and then turn out onto a large serving plate. When cool enough, work through couscous with the hands, making sure there are no clumps, lifting and letting it fall through the fingers. It should be fluffy and soft but not mushy, and should have expanded a few times in size. Sprinkle with essence of orange blossom, add in date cubes and ground nuts, and mix well with the hands. Slowly drizzle in half of the syrup, working in with the hands. The couscous should be moist but not soggy.

Transfer to a large serving platter. Form the grains into a mound. Dust with cinnamon and confectioners' sugar. Cut the remaining dates in half lengthwise. Decorate with date halves and whole nuts. Put remaining syrup in a small pitcher for those who want their couscous sweeter. Serve with glasses of cold milk or buttermilk.

Becherovka

FRANCINE PROSE

My love affair with Becherovka began in Prague, in the summer of 1994, when the afterglow of the Velvet Revolution was still investing the particulate matter in the polluted air with a glittery fairy-dust sparkle. I'd come for a month to teach and to write about the city of Mozart and Kafka, and I was living with my family on a desolate, romantic edge of town, surrounded by decaying diplomatic villas and bordering the lunar landscape of an abandoned-looking technical university. All of this hovered beneath the shadow of a grim, high-rise, Soviet-era hotel where, it was rumored, KGB agents tossed recalcitrant guests from the upper windows. The streetlights had a sensor system that had been installed backward so that the lights blazed constantly but blinked out as you approached them.

One night, I was invited to give a reading at the Globe bookstore, then a center for the arty expatriates and yuppie entrepreneurs drawn to the city by its beauty, its inexpensive apartments, and the Wild West feel of its position on the frontier between the past and the future. Some kind soul, imagining that I might be nervous about reading, suggested that I fortify myself with a drink of a special Czech liqueur.

A shot glass of syrupy honey-colored liquid arrived at my table. I took a sip, then another. It was like drinking liquid gold, though perhaps I only thought so because the effect of Becherovka is not only euphoric but slightly psychedelic. By the time I went up to the podium to read, a Becherovka-tinted light suffused the room, crowning each member of the audience with an individual halo. It struck me that I had never before seen such beautiful, interesting, charming people. In the first blush of my passion for Becherovka, I realized, beyond any doubt, that I had never been so wildly, so profoundly happy, and already I regretted all the glum, wasted hours of my pre-Becherovka life.

Among Becherovka's many charms are the beauty and oddness of its presentation. It comes in a tall, flat, dark green bottle, banded with a label emblazoned in primary colors (red, yellow, blue) and marked with a mysterious red seal. Everything about the extremely old-fashioned packaging exudes a sort of Imperial Hapsburg aura that goes hand in hand with the delightful paradox of an eighty-proof beverage doing a convincing impersonation of the sort of health tonic that might be prescribed for dyspepsia or sluggish blood or some other arcane diagnosis that only exists in Eastern Europe.

In fact, as the company's Web site (www.becherovka.cz) explains, the brew began as "digestive drops" concocted collaboratively by a Czech pharmacist named Josef Becher and a certain Englishman named Dr. Frobrig, the personal physician of Imperial Count Pletenberg-Mietingen. The Count had come to Karlovy Vary in 1807 to take the curative waters, and, as luck would have it, stayed at Becher's home, the House of the Three Skylarks.

Originally sold in small glass medicine bottles, Carlsbad English Bitter grew increasingly popular until 1841, when Josef left his business—together with his secret formula—to his son Johann. In the 1870s, Johann began to mass-produce his father's discovery, and approved the design of the bottle, which is still in use today. After World War II, the company was nationalized, but then returned to private ownership in 1997. All of this information can, I imagine, be found in the Jan

Becher Museum in Karlovy Vary, to which true devotees can, if they wish, make a sentimental pilgrimage.

Understandably, the Web site is considerably less forthcoming about the magical recipe: "These days, only two persons at the Karlovy Vary factory know the whole secret of Becherovka production, and it is unlikely that the company will disclose it any time soon. These two chosen people are the only ones who may enter the room called the 'Drogikamr,' a name used since the Bechers' time. Once a week, they prepare the mixture from many kinds of herbs and spices. About three-fourths of the herbs and spices come from abroad; some selected kinds grow in the vicinity of Karlovy Vary."

And just in case we are planning to torture the Drogikamr meisters into revealing their secret, or to analyze the formula and attempt to reproduce its chemistry in our own home labs or kitchen distilleries, we might as well spare ourselves the trouble. For apparently science has proved that Karlovy Vary itself exerts "a mysterious effect" on the taste of the liqueur: "Once, an experiment was made when the herb extracts were prepared at the Karlovy Vary plant and then moved to another place, where the beverage was manufactured using an identical technological procedure. The result? It was not Becherovka!"

After all these years, I can't say that I've gotten one step closer to fathoming what transpires inside the occult and closely guarded confines of the Drogikamr. And I can't help wondering if the FDA or the Bureau of Alcohol, Tobacco, Firearms and Explosives, or whatever government agency might be involved, does either. I'd guess that there's a heavy cinnamon component to the recipe, and certainly enough sugar so that I sometimes fear that drinking Becherovka for more than a decade might be the equivalent of attacking my own liver with a pneumatic drill. But like so many excesses, every guilty pleasure, the result—that mysterious sense of golden well-being—has always seemed well worth whatever damage I might be incurring.

By the end of that summer in Prague, my Becherovka habit was already so advanced that when at last it was time to go home, I emptied my suitcase and filled it with bottles of Becherovka, which, because of their flatness, pack extremely well. And after that, every time that I heard that someone—a friend, or a friend of a friend, or a friend of a friend of a friend—was traveling to Prague, I'd beg or cajole or somehow bribe the traveler into promising to bring me back a bottle. It was, I discovered, impossible to get here, though I searched for it everywhere in the mournful but eternally hopeful way you might search for a long-lost lover of whose whereabouts you had unaccountably lost track.

Consolingly, the Web site informed me that privatization was in progress and was expected to be completed by 2001. And, in fact, perseverance furthered. I now know of three liquor stores in downtown Manhattan where Becherovka can be bought, and I've prevailed upon my local wine merchant in the country to carry it. So I can only assume it can be found by anyone who wants to make the effort. Doubtless, this increased availability has something to do with the fact that Becherovka has been acquired, and is now distributed by, Pernod Ricard.

But in contrast to so many affairs, my romance with Becherovka has not been diminished by the passage of time, by accessibility or familiarity. In fact, I can't seem to forget or out-grow that anxious period during which I feared that I might not be able to get more. These days, I still buy two bottles at once, just in case . . .

In the spirit of jolly experimentalism, the Becherovka Web site lists the recipes for several terrifying-sounding cocktails. One of them, for example, suggests that the liqueur be mixed with the cola drink of your choice. Another is bright blue. But I've found that Becherovka is best served straight up and ice-cold, right out of the freezer. And one shot—to be taken nightly—is really all it takes (even for those with a reasonably hearty tolerance for alcohol) to be ushered directly into that marvelously altered state of consciousness that the drink can induce. A second dose is usually, I've discovered through sad experience, a gigantic mistake.

And Becherovka is not for everyone. I've served it (often with some hesitation) to quite a few friends, and many of them think it's positively disgusting. Too sweet, too unctuous, too strange. Even when my kids were teenagers, I knew that I could keep a bottle in the house and that neither they nor their most adventurous pals would make the smallest dent in my supply, despite the serious buzz that it would have provided. Perhaps that was yet another positive side effect of the medicinal-looking bottle.

But Becherovka has its fans, and they are devoted. Some years ago, when I asked a Czech friend about it, she sighed deeply, and a distant, rather dreamy look came into her eyes.

"It's a godsend," she said. "A lifesaver. I don't know what we would have done without it." Evidently, the healing powers of Becherovka had helped my friend and her family through some of the most stressful periods of the Russian occupation and Communist-era totalitarianism.

Which seems like yet another reason not to let my own supply dwindle too low. If our country continues any further in the political direction in which it seems to be headed, I intend to avail myself of what the Czechs discovered before the Velvet Revolution, long before my own relationship with the liqueur began: Becherovka's consolations, and the many adaptive, healthful uses of the tonic that Dr. Frobrig and Josef Becher concocted almost two hundred years ago.

The Apple of Their Eyes

SARA PERRY

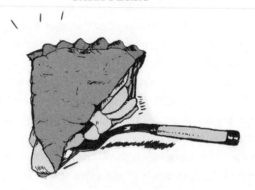

In the beginning, seeking perfection, Eve chose the apple. Smooth, round, fitting her palm, the apple's first luscious bite revealed a divine texture and heavenly taste. So ended Eve and Adam's sojourn in paradise.

Despite the fact that the apple of the Garden of Eden was probably a peach or a pomegranate—translators misunderstood the Hebrew word *tappauch*—the apple's connection with the mythological continued, provoking wars and erotic encounters. Eventually, a search for a different kind of perfection began, one that embraced the apple and created a culinary metamorphosis. Speaking more humbly, this was the search for the perfect apple pie, a pursuit shared by thousands of nameless souls, by myself, and by three extraordinary literary personalities whom I used as my guides.

I like the exotic. Apple pie needn't be humbled by its down-to-earth nature and its simple ingredients. Alice B. Toklas, the apple of Gertrude Stein's provocative eye, proved this beyond doubt with a rich, single-crusted pie that was filled with a wine-infused purée, then embellished like a cake with a rum-butter icing.

"A rose is a rose is a rose," Gertrude would say (and Alice would embroider the line as small as a rose hip on handkerchiefs), but an apple pie in Alice's Parisian kitchen was certainly a departure from the expected.

In the decades between the First and Second World Wars, Stein and Toklas's avant-garde salon was a gathering place for painters, sculptors, and writers. Stein befriended many, including Matisse, Picasso, and Hemingway, providing them with good food, wit, and conversation. To the world, she was the writer and the genius and Toklas was her Cerberus, guarding her privacy while bouncing bores, creating feasts, and talking to the wives.

Toklas could read a recipe and a person with equal aplomb, judging the strengths and weaknesses of each. Hemingway didn't fare too well; she thought he was a braggart. (In return, Hemingway never mentioned her name in *A Moveable Feast*, referring only to "Miss Stein and a companion.") In the kitchen, Toklas delighted in tasting a dish and unraveling the ingredients and techniques that made it special.

She was a remarkable woman in her own right. She had a sharp mind and a quick tongue. The author of two cookbooks, she had brusque opinions on the proper way to write a recipe. A New York editor, reviewing her second manuscript, queried the omission of serving amounts. She received a bristling response from Alice: "How should I know how many it serves? It depends—on their appetites—what else they have for dinner—whether they like it or not." (Did I mention she was quite sensible?)

As a young woman raised in San Francisco in the early 1900s, Toklas undoubtedly enjoyed the American standard, two-crusted, sliced-apple pie, but when she moved to France in her thirties, she came under the spell of continental cuisine and those sublime French tarts. That's when she began to cook in earnest, and her inventive mind went to work as she filled a buttery-rich *pâte brisée* (short-crust) with slowly simmered apple-wine essence.

What reads like applesauce-in-a-crust turns out to be an elegant yet simple dessert. Cut into sweet slivers, it's a startling confection. A woman who could be called plain, yet who dressed fashionably and wore remarkable hats, Toklas knew how to top off this culinary ensemble. She decked it with a potent, hard-sauce-style icing, making it the perfect pie for a Christmas or holiday feast. This is *not* a pie for a lost generation, and neither is her timely advice on cooking:

Use only the best the market offers. If the budget is restricted, restrict the menu to what the budget affords. Cook with the very best butter, draw on your best wines. ... This will exalt your effort, stimulate, intensify, indeed magnify the flavor.

The delectable perfume and enticing sweetness of an apple has always aroused our senses. Neolithic man found the glorious globe a scrumptious treat. Ancient Egyptians planted orchards to ensure its constant supply, and by 200 BC, the Romans were cultivating up to seven varieties. Today, there are two to three thousand varieties suitable for commercial growing, although supermarkets tend to carry only a dozen or so varieties that store well, stack well, and taste good. Regional farmers' markets and roadside stands are where the more unusual varieties can be bought and sampled.

Once you find a great-tasting apple, will it make the perfect pie? Not always. Some varieties, when cooked, lose their shape but are great for applesauce; others make terrific juice. Since it's not something you can tell by a look or a squeeze, ask the produce person for advice. Once you find the right pie apple and nestle it in a flaky crust, get ready to enjoy the quintessential comfort food and savory symbol of domestic bliss.

Some say apples and a pastry crust are like love and marriage. I think they're like love and sex: you can have one without the other, but it's better to have both. Erskine Caldwell, once one of the most widely read twentieth-century American authors, had firsthand knowledge of sex and a very good idea of what makes a perfect apple pie.

In the 1940s, Caldwell was America's literary "big apple," selling more books than any other writer in American history. (By 1960, his books had sold more than sixty million copies.) He was one of the first writers to be mass-marketed in paperback—and to many of us of a certain age, he wrote our first flashlight-in-bed "dirty" book (*God's Little Acre* or *Tobacco Road*, take your pick). Caldwell's stories about the poor of the American South mixed social realism with sex and violence. Some thought his depiction of Dixie surpassed Faulkner's. (Faulkner himself believed Caldwell to be one of America's five greatest novelists.)

Born in 1903 in Georgia, the son of a poor Presbyterian preacher who moved his son and wife from church to church, ministering to sharecroppers, Caldwell witnessed the desperate lives of his characters and until the early 1930s struggled to make ends meet from his writing. In 1935, with the success of his play *Tobacco Road*, he became a celebrity. Soon after, he left his first wife, Helen, and their three children for Margaret Bourke-White, one of the country's most famous photographers. All of his relationships, including three more marriages, would be marred by jealousy, betrayal, infidelity, and rage.

In 1938, a small red volume entitled *A Stag at Ease* appeared. Margaret Squire had embarked on the lofty aim of publishing "the culinary preferences of a number of distinguished male citizens of the world." With Carl Sandburg's cheese omelet,

Jack Dempsey's macaroni and cheese, and A. A. Milne's crème brûlée, she was sure it would prove "a treasure trove for the hostess who aims to please."

Caldwell contributed a two-layer apple pie crust recipe, leaving the filling to be worked out by the reader. The kitchen is a revealing place, and Caldwell's omission is not so surprising from a man who saw the need to conceal and cover up. Whatever his motive, Caldwell's crust is a winner because instead of using butter for the fat and flavor, his recipe calls for shortening (for flakiness) and grated cheese (for flavor), which makes a lot of sense when you think about it. Cheese has always been a perfect partner for apple pie. "Apple pie without cheese," say the English, "is like a kiss without a squeeze."

Time and time again, in the lean years, Caldwell left his family to write in solitude, and his letters reveal a diet that consisted of bread, cheese, and water. It's what he could afford; it's what tasted good and filled his belly; it was his comfort food. With the sweet taste of success—and the request for a recipe—Caldwell proved an intuitive cook. For those of us who like both sex and love (or pie crust and apples), I recommend combining Caldwell's crust with a fine pie apple, such as Jonagold, and a good sauce apple, such as McIntosh.

While there are countless recipes for apple pie, most are simply instructions. A favorite recipe—a perfect recipe—is like a culinary diary that reflects a delicious taste, a comfortable place, or a wonderful moment.

Before the late eighteenth and early nineteenth centuries, when professional cookbooks became available, most recipes were part of individual collections, handed down from one generation to the next, recording favorite dishes from decades back. English novelist Jane Austen, whose stories bring alive early nineteenth-century middle-class life in England, depended on these recipes for her large and sociable family.

In Georgian times, dinner was often a lavish affair for friends and family. This mid- to late-afternoon meal might last for hours, with up to two dozen homemade dishes. Without today's refrigeration, providing the ingredients and cooking all this food was a consuming task. Staples such as fruits and vegetables were seasonal and usually homegrown.

The Austens had a family garden and a cellar or cold room, so that fruits such as apples and pears could be used year-round. While apples can be stored for months this way, the fragrant, delectable flavor quickly vanishes, as irrevocably as a golden autumn day. When making an apple pie, Jane and other cooks of her day wisely simmered the peels and cores to extract any nuance of flavor and used the liquid in the filling. They also relied on the tart and brilliant taste of lemon zest and the crush of spicy cinnamon to supply flavor when flavor was missing.

It may sound surprising, but in the fall and early winter, when I want to showcase apples at their peak, I go for Jane's pie every time. It's bottomless, so there's less crust to interfere with the taste of newly harvested apples. (I do cut back on the zest.) In the spring and summer months, when just-picked apples are only a memory but the longing for pie is immediate, her recipe is the one I crave. Then the lemony perfume seems just right.

Each of my guides—Alice, Erskine, and Jane—showed me very different, yet perfect apple pies. I think, in the kitchen, perfection is a mingling of many different ingredients: imagination, hunger, history, and experience. Like the writer, I suppose, the cook takes off where nature left off.

RECIPES

The recipes have been tested by the author from primary sources. They have been rewritten for today's cook and, if necessary, ingredient amounts have been prudently revised for successful results.

Pâte Brisée (short-crust pastry)

makes one 9-inch pie crust

INGREDIENTS:

1 cup all-purpose flour
Pinch of salt
½ cup (1 stick) cold, unsalted butter, cut into 8 pieces
About 3 tablespoons ice water, plus more if necessary

Combine flour and salt in food processor; pulse once. Add the butter and pulse until the mixture resembles coarse crumbs, about 10 seconds. Some of the butter chunks should still be the size of small peas. (This can also be done by hand, in a bowl with a pastry cutter, two forks, or your fingertips.)

Place mixture in bowl and sprinkle with 3 tablespoons water. Stir with a wooden spoon or rubber spatula and gather the mixture into a ball. If too dry, add another ½ tablespoon water. When you can gather the mixture into a ball with your hands, wrap it in plastic and flatten it into a small disk. Refrigerate for 30 minutes.

Sprinkle the counter with flour. Unwrap the dough and sprinkle with flour. (If the dough is too hard, let it rest for a few minutes until it gives a little when pressed with a finger.) For easy rolling, place the dough between two sheets of plastic wrap or inside a 2-gallon plastic freezer bag.

Roll from the center out. If dough seems sticky, dust with flour. Rotate dough and turn it over once or twice until the dough is about 10 inches in diameter and $1/_8$ inch thick.

Drape the dough over the rolling pin or fold into quarters. Place the dough into a 9-inch pie plate and press firmly into the bottom and sides. Trim the excess to about ½ inch all around, then tuck it under itself around the edge of the plate. Decorate the edge with fork or fingers. Refrigerate for 30 minutes.

Preheat the oven to 400 degrees. Line the pie plate with aluminum foil and fill it with dry beans. Bake for 15 minutes. Remove the beans and foil. Bake until the bottom of the shell is light golden, 10 to 15 minutes.

Jane Austen's Apple Pie

serves 6

INGREDIENTS:

1 9-inch *pâte brisée* (short-crust) pie shell, baked (see page 98)
2 pounds pie apples
½ cup water
½ cinnamon stick
4 tablespoons granulated sugar, divided
Grated zest of ½ small lemon
Softened butter as a garnish (optional)

Prepare the *pâte brisée* dough in advance. Preheat the oven to 400 degrees.

Peel and core the apples. Place the peels and cores in a saucepan. Add the water and bring the mixture to a boil over medium heat. Reduce to low and continue to simmer until the liquid tastes like apples, about 10 minutes. Strain the liquid and return it to the saucepan. Add the cinnamon stick and 2 tablespoons of the sugar and slowly boil until the mixture is reduced to 1/4 cup, about 10 minutes.

Meanwhile, roll out the pastry dough according to the recipe. Cut a 1-inch strip along the outside edge of the rolled-out pastry circle. Grease the rim of a 9-inch pie plate and gently press the pastry strip over it. Slice half of the apples and place them in the pie plate. Sprinkle with 1 tablespoon of sugar and half of the lemon zest. Slice the remaining apples and place them on top of the first layer. Sprinkle the remaining 1 tablespoon of sugar and the lemon zest over the apples.

Remove and discard the cinnamon stick from the reduced liquid and pour the liquid over the apples. Lightly moisten the top of the pastry strip with water and cover the filling with the reserved pastry circle. Trim off any excess. Press the crusts together with a fork and crimp to seal. Prick the top crust with the fork in several places. With a small sharp knife, cut several slits at right angles to each other between the center and edge of the crust and a small vent in the center.

Place the pie on a baking sheet and bake until the crust is browned and the juices bubble up through the slits, 35 to 40 minutes. Cool on a wire rack for 3 to 6 hours before serving. This allows the juices to thicken and the apples to reabsorb some of the juice. If desired, when eaten warm, place a slice of butter on the top.

Alice B. Toklas's Apple Pie

serves: Depends (says Alice)

INGREDIENTS:

2 ½ pounds fresh cooking apples, quartered, cored,
  peeled, and cut into chunks
½ cup granulated sugar
½ cup excellent red wine
1 9-inch *pâte brisée* (short-crust) pie shell, baked (see
  page 98)
1 ½ cups powdered sugar
4 tablespoons unsalted butter
2 to 3 tablespoons good pale rum
Water for thinning

Place the apples in a large, heavy pot. Cover and cook over low heat, stirring with a wooden spoon, until the apples are very tender, about 30 minutes.

Uncover the pot and stir in the sugar and wine. The apples will be soft and may still hold their shape. Turn the heat up to medium. Keep the mixture at a slow boil, stirring frequently until the apples cook down to a thick purée, 20 to 30 minutes. (To test the purée's thickness, run a spoon or a spatula along the pot's bottom. The purée should separate and remain apart for about 10 seconds.)

Remove the pot from the heat and let it cool. Run the purée through a food mill or processor until smooth and then chill. The filling can be made up to 3 days ahead for maximum flavor. Makes about 2 cups.

To make the icing, stir together the powdered sugar, butter, and rum to a creamy consistency, adding a little water if necessary.

To assemble, pour and spread the chilled purée into the baked pie shell. Pour and gently spread the icing over the filling. Let the icing set, about 20 minutes. Cut into small slices and serve.

Erskine Caldwell's Apple Pie

serves 6 to 8

INGREDIENTS:

Pastry

2 cups all-purpose flour

½ teaspoon salt

½ teaspoon granulated sugar

½ teaspoon baking powder

¾ cup cold shortening

1 cup cold, grated, sharp Cheddar cheese, such as Black Diamond or Vermont

4 tablespoons ice water, plus more if necessary

Filling

2 tablespoons unsalted butter
2 1/2 pounds (6 to 7 medium) Jonagold apples, cut, cored,
    peeled, and quartered
1/2 pound (2 medium) McIntosh apples, cut, cored,
    peeled, and quartered
1/2 cup granulated sugar
1/2 teaspoon ground cinnamon
Pinch of salt
1 teaspoon to 1 tablespoon lemon juice

To prepare the pastry dough, combine the flour, salt, sugar, and baking powder. Toss well to combine. Using a pastry blender, two knives, or your fingertips, cut the shortening into the mixture until it forms small clumps. (You can also do this in a food processor.) Toss in the cheese. Stir evenly to combine.

Sprinkle in the ice water. Stir with a wooden spoon or rubber spatula and gather the mixture into a ball. If too dry, dribble in more water. When you can gather the mixture with your hands, press it together to form a ball. Divide into two halves and wrap each half in plastic. Flatten each into small disks and refrigerate for at least 30 minutes.

To prepare the filling, heat the butter in a large skillet over medium-high heat. Add the apple slices, sugar, cinnamon, and salt. Once the apples begin to sizzle, turn the heat to low. Cover the pan and simmer the apples until the juices are released, about 8 minutes. The McIntoshes will begin to break down. Uncover and continue to cook over medium-high heat until the juices begin to thicken and the McIntoshes fall apart, about 5 minutes. Remove from heat and transfer the mixture to a bowl. Cool to room temperature. Add lemon juice to taste.

Preheat the oven to 400 degrees.

To roll out the crust, sprinkle a countertop with flour. Unwrap one portion of dough and sprinkle with flour. (If the dough is too hard, let it rest for a few minutes until it gives a little when pressed with a finger.) For easy rolling, place the dough between two sheets of plastic wrap or inside a 2-gallon plastic freezer bag.

Roll from the center out. If the dough seems sticky, dust with flour. Rotate and turn over once or twice until the dough is about 10 inches in diameter and $1/_8$ inch thick.

Drape the dough over the rolling pin. Place the dough into a 9-inch glass pie plate, pressing firmly into the bottom and sides. Trim the dough to ½-inch overhang. Add the cooled apple mixture, mounding and patting it slightly. Brush the edge of the bottom crust with water.

Roll out the remaining dough. Lay it over the apples. Trim the top and bottom edges to ½-inch overhang. Tuck so that the folded crust is flush with the lip. Press with fork tines to seal. Prick the top crust with the fork in several places. With a small sharp knife, cut several slits at right angles to each other between the center and edge of the crust, as well as a small vent in the center.

Place the pie on a baking sheet and bake for 15 minutes. Lower the heat to 350 degrees until the crust is browned and the juices bubble up through the slits, about 35 minutes. (You may need to protect the crust edges with foil during the last 10 minutes.) Cool on a wire rack for 30 minutes to 1 hour. Serve warm.

Variation: For cheese lovers, grate an additional 1 cup sharp Cheddar cheese and sprinkle it over the apple mixture before adding the top crust.

PIE APPLES

(apples that hold their shape and texture)

Braeburn, Cox Orange Pippin, Empire, Granny Smith
Jonathan, Jonagold, Northern Spy
Rhode Island Greening

SAUCE APPLES

(apples that have a soft texture for smooth sauces)

Cortland, Empire, Gravenstein, Jonathan, McIntosh
Northern Spy, Winesap

EATING APPLES

(crisp, juicy apples for luscious eating)

Braeburn, Empire, Fuji, Gala, Gravenstein
JonagoldMutsu, Northern Spy, Winesap

The Perfect Apple Pie Primer

~ Apples are at their best in the fall and early winter.

~ Choose the best, freshest, blemish-free apples available. Look for locally grown varieties.

~ Buy apples that are firm to the touch and use them within a few days.

~ Keep apples refrigerated or in a very cool place. A centerpiece of apples spilling out of a bowl may look great, but an apple's flavor fades fast when stored at room temperature.

~ To prepare several apples at one time, it's easiest to use a paring knife to cut each apple in quarters, then remove the core and the peel.

~ Prevent peeled apples from turning brown by placing them in a bowl of lemon water. (1 quart water, juice of 1 lemon). Dry slices on a paper towel before using in a recipe.

~ Cut apple wedges into 1/4-inch slices to hold their shape and texture while baking.

~ 4 small, 3 medium, or 2 large apples yield one pound of apples.

~ One pound of apples yields 4 cups of sliced apples, 1 1/2 cups applesauce, or 3/4 cup purée.

~ Apple pie in July? Sure, but not from local apples. Look in the market for apples from New Zealand, where winter is just beginning. Braeburns are a good choice.

Ode to an Egg

MICHELLE WILDGEN

On this morning there was brioche and red raspberry preserve and the eggs were boiled and there was a pat of butter that melted as they stirred them and salted them lightly and ground pepper over them in the cups. They were big eggs and fresh and the girl's were not cooked quite as long as the young man's. . . . He was happy with his which he diced up with the spoon and ate with only the flow of the butter to moisten them.

—ERNEST HEMINGWAY

The Garden of Eden was not a good book, but I was so busy reading Hemingway's descriptions of food, especially eggs, that it took me several years to notice. Like so many things, the book begins with eggs. As newlyweds, Hemingway informs us, the Bournes eat them each morning, excited just to contemplate the manner of cooking them. The husband never abandons his joyful consumption of *oeufs au jambon* and eventually finds happiness in love and work. The wife begins to skip breakfast about midway through. Things turn out badly for her.

Probably one of the most private things in the world is an egg until it is broken.

—M. F. K. Fisher

In English the word *egg* is something to cup in one's palm. On the page, the extra *g*, like a linguistic wink, lends the word the same oblong shape as the thing itself. *Egg* nestles against the curve of the tongue.

In its shell it is all smoothness and balance. Next to it, other kinds of beauty seem bony and embellished, and at times I think the nutmeg speckling on a blue egg is as much as we can hope for. Yet the egg lends its beauty generously—witness the way egg tempera allows itself to be saturated with color; the chalky aura that bathes a Vermeer, as though the painter has cast his light through a broken shell.

M. F. K. Fisher mused that the egg is privacy itself. As a metaphor for self-containment, only the oyster comes close, but its rough-ribboned shell lacks the egg's tranquility. The oyster must clamp itself closed, while the egg simply has not noticed anyone else.

I had an excellent repast—the best repast possible— which consisted simply of boiled eggs and bread and butter. It was the quality of these simple ingredients that made the occasion memorable. The eggs were so good that I am ashamed to say how many of them I consumed. . . . It might seem that an egg which has succeeded in being fresh has done all that can reasonably be expected of it. But there was a bloom of punctuality, so to speak, about these eggs of Bourg, as if it had been the intention of the very hens themselves that they should be promptly served.

—Henry James

Those of us who did not grow up on farms retain some idealism about a fresh egg. I used to buy mine from a silent old man at a Wisconsin farmers' market whose hand-lettered signs promised brown eggs, duck eggs, ayacuna eggs in yellow, pink, and blue pastels, and, if you would ask, the story of his unjust accusations and upcoming trial. He disappeared from the market, though his stand remained, staffed by children who looked to be about eleven, so I kept buying his eggs. They were smaller than supermarket eggs, each one about the size of a new potato. Bits of sticky hay clung to the shells, and the yolks were a rich orange-gold. I fed them to my skeptical mother and made a convert out of her.

~~~~~~~~~~~~~~~~~~~~~~~~~~~

I can suck melancholy out of a song as a weasel sucks eggs.

—Shakespeare, *As You Like It*

A hen is only an egg's way of making another egg.

—Samuel Butler

The Oxford Companion to Food calls the egg an "unintentional gift," which is a self-deceiving way of saying we steal them. In other animals such behavior seems especially rapacious, not to mention sneaky. The dinosaur known as *oviraptor* ("egg thief") got its name when its skeleton was discovered on a cache of fossilized eggs. Scientists assumed the dinosaur was stealing them rather than warming them and christened it accordingly. Misunderstood or not, such a creature lacks grandeur. It seems poor sport to eat the unborn. The killers we most admire—the tigers, the grizzlies—are the John Waynes of the animal world. They have no need to assume the creepy delicacy of a mongoose slithering into the henhouse.

But we humans, sly lot, are the greatest oviraptors of all, and we will never admit it. We'll never compare ourselves to the mongoose or the weasel, because it might turn our egg-love into something that feels prurient and deceitful. We believe we are in it for commerce or gourmandise, that the matter-of-fact hand beneath the hen is retrieving only what it's owed, or that the pleasure in pearls of caviar bursting against the roofs of our mouths is near-godly delectation.

We are kidding ourselves, of course; the delight we feel at the discovery of an unexpected cluster of eggs is pure animal gratitude for protein, for succulence, for easy pickings. The beachcomber who unearths a clutch of leathery turtle eggs warmed in the sand, the diner who finds a cache of scarlet pearls upon cracking the lobster shell, and the fisherman who slices open a sturgeon to discover the black burst fruit of its roe all treat the discovery as though it were a pile of gold coins. When it comes to an egg, any egg, humans are pure avarice. Hence, the egg is an animal's most vulnerable possession. The egg is its secret.

~~~~~~~~~~~~~~~~~~~~~~~~~~~~~

The love of eggs is a love for the tiny and tender—pinkie-sized squash, potatoes like marbles, three-week-old chickens, skinny-limbed lambs and calves—but taken one step backward. To us it feels wholesome, as though there is no kinder thing on earth than to give someone a plate of eggs, but every now and again you get a reminder of what you're dealing with. You crack a shell and find the freak egg: the yellow sphere inexplicably twinned like a biology experiment, a bloody vein buried in the meat of the yolk.

~~~~~~~~~~~~~~~~~~~~~~~~~~~~~

Eggs are very much like small boys. If you overheat them, or overbeat them, they will turn on you, and no amount of future love will right the wrong.

—Anonymous

As befits a thing of pure potential, the egg's versatility is unparalleled. Americans cooking at home don't test this versatility as much as we might, aware that—probably in punishment for our invasion—the egg doesn't lend itself to careless treatment. Faced with gracelessness, an egg asserts itself. Whip up mayonnaise in the food processor instead of the more gentle blender and the gluey result is most likely just what the egg thinks you deserve. Subject a custard to unmitigated heat without its water bath and·see how it likes that. Just try skipping the tempering of beaten yolks with warm liquid before adding them to a béarnaise and watch the egg clench its proteins like fists. You will be no more successful with a chilly egg yanked from the fridge than you will with a date you have shoved into a swimming pool. It's no surprise we get our word *coddle* from the treatment of an egg. An egg demands a little respect before it yields itself, loosens up its silky insides, and draws its neighbors in.

But once granted a little kindness, the egg is the workhorse of the culinary world. Its greatest talent is to deliver other flavors while retaining its own. A scrambled egg's yolky flavor is the cushion on which chives or truffle oil lay themselves. A soufflé is no spongy messenger, but the medium itself, lending its unmistakable flavor—it can only be called *eggy*—to cheese and chocolate alike. The whites whip up to glossy peaks more lovely and ephemeral than flower blossoms. But white and yolks are yin and yang, achieving more significance together than apart. Beaten together they become creamy and thick, a sweet butter-yellow that would cheer any depressive.

The best of us are fools for omelets. The insipid egg-white omelet, which strangles its filling in rubbery proteins, does not count. The real thing is delicate, spongy, light, and sunny yellow, laced with butter and a sprinkling of cheese. I have never mastered the classic trifolded French omelet, and I remain convinced this is attributable to using the wrong pan. (I am fooling myself; I will have to work harder. The pretentious word *technique* suddenly seems appropriate.) Most of us have consumed innumerable omelets, but not many have had a really good one. I know I have eaten omelets that oozed strange juice, bore burned spots that stayed in my teeth like bitter leaves. The proliferation of the egg-white omelet allowed us to convince ourselves that an omelet is health food. It isn't. It shouldn't be. I ate hundreds of veggie egg-white omelets before admitting they resembled broccoli stuck to the bottom of a shoe.

I probably should have refused them, but, faced even with an inferior omelet, I always try.

~~~~~~~~~~~~~~~~~~~~~~~~~~~~

An egg is always an adventure; the next one may be different.

—Oscar Wilde

Raw, they nourish the hungover; cooked, they nourish everyone. At a potluck a few years ago, I and a dozen other wine-snob gourmands abandoned our homemade foccaccia and shrimp pot stickers and stormed the deviled eggs someone had made as a joke. The egg is childhood—urban, suburban, and rural alike. This explains why omelets, frittatas, and Spanish tortillas are mainstays rather than special-occasion dishes. Yet the egg's seeming good nature also explains the occasional misstep, such as at a farm breakfast I once attended in Sheboygan, Wisconsin, where dozens of eggs were stirred up and cooked in a huge, shallow tin bowl like a hubcap over some pallid coals and then spooned onto our plates in runny clumps. This strikes me as an experience that could have been avoided.

But when dealings with an egg are successful, there is nothing quite like it. When my husband had his wisdom teeth out, I gave him chicken broth with finely chopped spinach. It occurred to me to try whisking beaten eggs into the hot liquid, and in a minute they formed a loose golden net suspended in the broth. This is an age-old idea, but right then it felt like genius. I felt strangely capable and nourishing, like a farmwife, but sexy. Eggs will do that to you. Something similar happened when I made béarnaise (breaking it on the first try, whipping in more clarified butter until it gathered itself together again), except that time I felt rather cool and daring, as though I were descended from the French Resistance rather than Alsatian peasant stock.

The egg is sophistication and breakfast all at once. A friend who worked in a hip restaurant once served me scrambled eggs with truffle oil and porcinis at midnight on a Saturday. I was sitting at the blond-wood bar, dabbing with my toast at the soft curds of cooked egg and slicing through a fat porcini stem. Elsewhere at the bar, people were smoking cigars and drinking flights of champagne or Italian reds. I had a white burgundy because it went nicely with the truffle and the egg and as I did it struck me that wine with breakfast was not a bad idea. Not a bad idea at all.

"Only women order this dish," the bartender informed me. "It's too sexy for the men."

Until then, "sexy" was never one of the adjectives I would have ascribed to an egg. The egg is drama and succor, birth and parenthood, sex and death, the start and the finish. The egg is inevitable.

RECIPE

Eggs with Mushrooms and Truffles

A note on ingredients: This is as costly as you wish to make it, depending on the types of mushrooms and truffles you choose. I would gladly use fresh chanterelles, porcini, or any other exotic mushroom, but usually content myself with a mix of button, cremini, and shiitakes instead. As for the truffles, many food lovers insist that truffle oil should be shunned in favor of the real, precious fresh fungi at all costs. Such people fill me with rage and envy, but not, sadly, with truffles. I say find a good truffle oil and pay your rent on time. Lastly and most importantly, the eggs. They really must be the good ones, free-range organic if possible, the sort with bright orange, rich yolks, not the supermarket ones. Farmers' markets often have these eggs, the best stand usually recognizable by the long line of people gazing dreamily toward the sky and clutching sweaty five-dollar bills. Join them.

serves 2

INGREDIENTS:

4–5 eggs
4 tablespoons unsalted butter
1–2 tablespoons cream or half-and-half, optional
1 pound mushrooms, made up of any combination of
    button, cremini, shiitake, or other wild mushroom,
    washed and sliced
White truffle oil
Salt and pepper

Have all ingredients at room temperature.

Heat 2 tablespoons butter over medium heat, then add mushrooms and toss to coat. They will soak up the fat almost instantly, but keep stirring and they'll release it again in a few minutes. Let the mushrooms cook, stirring occasionally, for 5 minutes or so, then season with salt and pepper, turn off heat, and cover them to keep them warm.

Beat the eggs lightly with a fork, just enough to blend. Meanwhile, heat 2 to 3 tablespoons of butter over the lowest heat possible—some even say over a double boiler. When butter is melted and slightly foamy, pour in the eggs and cream, if using, and get comfortable. Using a wooden spoon (the sort with a flat tip would be perfect here), stir the eggs slowly and constantly. Keep doing this till the eggs have set in soft curds, which may take 15 or 20 minutes. Resist the temptation to turn up the heat. When they are set, still tender, but not dry, divide eggs and mushrooms between two plates. Drizzle the mushrooms and eggs with truffle oil. It's heady stuff, so go easy. Season to taste with salt and freshly ground pepper. This dish is especially good with toast and spinach sautéed in butter.

Here's to Crime!

DAVID LEHMAN

Breeze looked at me very steadily. Then he sighed. Then he picked the glass up and tasted it and sighed again and shook his head sideways with a half smile, the way a man does when you give him a drink and he needs it very badly and it is just right and the first swallow is like a peek into a cleaner, sunnier, brighter world.

The writer is Raymond Chandler, the book *The High Window* (1942), and the narrator Philip Marlowe, the gumshoe Galahad who has just sociably mixed a drink for a cop. Not a very exotic drink either, but an ordinary highball (ginger ale, ice cubes, and a shot of rye whiskey): a drink once ubiquitous, now hopelessly passé. Yet it brings out the lyric poet in Chandler, who had studied his Hemingway and knew that a succession of terse clauses connected by the commonest of conjunctions can produce sublime effects.

The hard-boiled detective novel came into being during the raucous last years of Prohibition, and the genre is soaked in whiskey, sinfulness, and the dark—as if time had stopped during a New Year's Eve of the soul at 4 AM when the celebration has subsided and someone has to go around picking up the pieces. The detective in the works of Chandler, Dashiell Hammett, and their successors is a hard-drinking man, a loner who may not have a secretary but assuredly has a bottle of hooch in the desk drawer and a flask in his hip pocket, and he reaches for one or the other when bad news hits. In an early chapter of *The Maltese Falcon* (1930), Hammett's Sam Spade gets a middle-of-the-night phone call informing him of his partner's violent death. During the next fifty minutes, Spade smokes exactly five cigarettes and downs three wine glasses full of Bacardi.

Spade's drinking and smoking mark him as a more ambiguous hero than any official guardian of the law. Yes, in the end he does the right thing, but you can never be sure of this unpredictable and even somewhat satanic fellow with the Camel dangling from his lower lip and the glass of rum in his hand.

For all the booze consumed in Hammett's *The Thin Man*, where sleuths Nick and Nora Charles are awash in Scotch and water, Chandler is really the king of the cocktails. Philip Marlowe without a drink is very nearly as unthinkable as Humphrey Bogart—who played Sam Spade in the movie version of *The Maltese Falcon* (1941) and Marlowe in *The Big Sleep* (1946)—without fedora, trench coat, and unfiltered cigarette. Some of Marlowe's drinking is compulsive, yet it brings him a certain sardonic pleasure. A chapter of *The Lady in the Lake* (1943) begins with Marlowe regaining consciousness after a blow to the head: "I smelled of gin. Not just casually, as if I had taken four or five drinks of a winter morning to get out of bed on, but as if the Pacific Ocean was pure gin and I had nosedived off the boat deck." A chapter later he is thirsty again. "I went back to the whiskey decanter and did what I could about being too sober," he cracks.

"One must always be drunk," Charles Baudelaire wrote in one of his prose poems, and Marlowe, who does his best to heed this advice, resembles the figure Baudelaire calls the "stranger"—a man alienated from friends, family, religion, and patriotism, who reserves his love for the "passing clouds." But though Marlowe doesn't mind drinking alone, he also revels in the cocktail hour as a social ritual, regardless of the venue. No accident that in *Farewell, My Lovely* (1940), Marlowe's tone-setting first meeting with his client—the oversized, loudly dressed Moose Malloy, who is "about as inconspicuous as a tarantula on a slice of angel food"—takes place in a cheerless bar where the two men drink whiskey sours.

Chandler was very particular about his drinks and liked switching favorites from book to book. In *The Lady in the Lake*, a "wizened waiter with evil eyes and a face like a gnawed bone" serves Marlowe a Bacardi cocktail—we'd probably call it a daiquiri (juice of one lime, two shots of rum, sugar). By the time of *Playback* (1958), Chandler's last book, Marlowe has begun to favor double Gibsons (gin and vermouth as in a martini, but with a cocktail onion substituted for the olive or lemon twist).

Chandler liked gimlets so much, he included a recipe in *The Long Goodbye* (1953). In the book, Marlowe and his pal Terry Lennox make a habit of meeting at Victor's and drinking gimlets. "What they call a gimlet is just some lime or lemon juice and gin with a dash of sugar and bitters," Lennox says scornfully. "A real gimlet is half gin and half Rose's Lime Juice and nothing else. It beats martinis hollow." (I, a lover of summer cocktails, never enjoyed the full savor of a gimlet until I followed this recipe to the letter.) Yet even the flawed gimlets at Victor's do the trick: "I like to watch the man mix the first one of the evening and put it down on a crisp mat and put the little folded napkin beside it. I like to taste it slowly. The first quiet drink of the evening in a quiet bar."

From the point of view of crafting prose and managing transitions, the cocktail is a great prop in Chandler's hands. The offer of a drink can lubricate a reluctant witness ("a guy that buys me a drink is a pal"), pacify a cop, or romance a frail. Drinking cocktails is how Marlowe gets from one chapter to another, from the bar at the casino or nightclub—some flashy place that "looked like a high-budget musical. A lot of light and glitter, a lot of scenery, a lot of clothes, a lot of sound, an all-star cast, and a plot with all the originality and drive of a split fingernail"—to the back office where a tough guy in a double-breasted suit tries to buy him or threaten him off the case.

Think of all the bridge sentences in which a cocktail figures in Chandler's novels. You can convey the atmosphere of the narrative, if not the narrative itself, from a loose assortment of them. "I carried the drink over to a small table against the wall and sat down there and lit a cigarette." "It made my head feel worse but it made the rest of me feel better." "He finished his drink at a gulp and stood up." "I liked him better drunk." "Then you cracked me on the head with a whiskey bottle." "He lifted the empty glass and brought it down hard on the edge of the table." "I finished my drink and went after him." "His whiskey sour hadn't seemed to improve his temper." "I needed a drink badly and the bars were closed." It sounds like a noirish prose poem.

The cocktail shared with a person of either sex is an expression of real or spurious intimacy in Hammett and Chandler. The first sign of betrayal is a doctored drink, as when the Fat Man slips Sam Spade a Mickey in *The Maltese Falcon*. The most popular toast in detective fiction generally is "Here's to crime," or "Success to crime," though Chandler gets off a beauty in *The Big Sleep* (1939), his first novel, in the scene in which the thug gets ready to administer a fatal dose of poison to a luckless but honorable small-time crook: "Moths in your ermine, as the ladies say." The character of old General Sternwood, Marlowe's client in *The Big Sleep*, is delineated in dialogue centering precisely on what the two men are, or are not, drinking. Sitting in a greenhouse, wrapped in a heavy bathrobe, the general is now belatedly paying the price for a dissipated life. No longer allowed to drink, he nostalgically recalls that he used to take his brandy "with champagne. The champagne as cold as Valley Forge and about a third of a glass of brandy beneath it." Marlowe enjoys his drink ("brandy and soda") and his cigarette, and the general enjoys watching. "A nice state of affairs when a man has to indulge his vices by proxy," the old man says "dryly," a most apt adverb. If the Scotch and sodas in Hammett's *The Thin Man* signal sophistication, the cocktails in Chandler seem to stand for virility.

Though the drinking is much more measured in the classic detective story as practiced by Dorothy Sayers or Agatha Christie, both authors use alcoholic references to help establish the character of their detective heroes. Sayers has a story, "The Bibulous Business of a Matter of Taste," in which two men claiming to be Lord Peter Wimsey are asked to prove it in a wine-tasting competition. Wimsey, the resourceful patrician pleased with his own cleverness, is naturally a connoisseur of fine French wines—and proves his identity by unerringly telling a Chevalier-Montrachet 1911 from a Montrachet-Aine of the same year. In Christie's Hercule Poirot novels, the great detective's love of aperitifs, like his waxed mustache, his French name, and his hobby of growing artichokes, distinguishes him from the rest of the cast. We're never allowed to forget that Poirot is a foreigner as well as an eccentric. With a hopeful air, he seems always to be offering the Scotland Yard inspector a variety of cordials—crème de menthe, Benedictine, crème de cacao—and is forever disappointed when the beefy British policeman chooses British beer. The theme of English xenophobia, always present beneath the surface, is an unexpected point of interest in Christie's novels.

Many have commented on the haute cuisine in Rex Stout's detective novels. Fewer have noticed the sometimes strategic use to which the novelist puts beverages. Stout's sleuth is Nero Wolfe, a man of pure mind and seemingly unfunctional body. He is huge, perhaps the fattest detective in a genre full of fat detectives, and he rarely vacates his armchair except to tend his prize orchids. The legwork is done by Archie Goodwin, Wolfe's right-hand man, who is dashing and charming if always one mental step behind Wolfe, as befits a narrator in the Sherlock Holmes-Dr. Watson tradition. A running gag is that he-man Archie guzzles milk while egghead Wolfe pours down the beer, pitchers of the stuff.

Archie may drink milk the way my Toyota drinks gasoline, for fuel. But he knows how to behave when it's cocktail time, and so does Wolfe's client Mrs. Bruner in *The Doorbell Rang*

(1965). Archie has taken the attractive woman to lunch at a fancy midtown restaurant. His opinion of her improves when she orders, and enjoys, "a double dry martini with onion"—he had guessed her for Dubonnet or sherry, and no onion. He has a martini himself, he tells us, to "keep her company." One reason I like *The Doorbell Rang* so much is that a vital clue is a young woman's appropriation (and revision) of some lines in Keats's "Ode on a Grecian Urn." Another reason is that I first read the novel in 1972, the year of Watergate, and the book's plot has a lot to do with illegal wiretaps and abuses of power in high places. A third reason is that one suspect's alibi is that she was attending a lecture at the New School on Twelfth Street at the time of the murder. I teach there but cannot corroborate her story.

It could be said that cocktails figure in detective fiction the way they figure in urban life. But there is another explanation for the significance of the cocktail in thrillers. George Simenon, the creator of Jules Maigret, the introspective French inspector with a penchant for a pipe and an aperitif or two in a café, came to the United States to live for a time after World War II. He stopped drinking wine with his meals and instead drank cocktails before them: "Manhattan after Manhattan, then dry Martini after dry Martini." He had always enjoyed drinking but never before felt like an alcoholic. "From one end of the country to the other there exists a freemasonry of alcoholics," he remarked. It is possible that the hard-boiled detective novel, the noir movie, and even the comic thriller derive some of their energy from the national American fellowship of alcoholism.

You can read Hitchcock's *North by Northwest* (1959) as a progress away from alcoholism toward redemption. The hero played by Cary Grant is, when the film begins, an advertising man with a domineering mother and a drinking problem. The movie hops from one locale to another, and a way to keep track is through the drinks he either has or orders: martinis with business associates at the Plaza, the bottle of bourbon force-fed him by the bad guys in the Long Island estate, a Gibson on the train with Eva Marie Saint, Scotch in her hotel room, and more bourbon after the fake shooting at Mount Rushmore. This sequence of drinks is seemingly indiscriminate and would be indigestible, which is part of the point, but it's noteworthy that he doesn't drink the bourbon he asks for after the fake shooting—it's a ruse to get rid of an unwanted character. In the course of his adventures, Cary Grant has graduated from his dependencies and, at the end, has Eva Marie Saint in his arms to show for it. But then he is Cary Grant. More common in the literature and film of detection is the unreformed alcoholic who celebrates the state of intoxication. When Nora asks Nick in *The Thin Man*, "Why don't you stay sober today?" he answers for all the detectives in the hard-boiled tradition: "We didn't come to New York to stay sober."

The drinking of cocktails in a crummy bar in Los Angeles or a swell speakeasy on West Fifty-second Street is like the renewal of life itself to these creatures of night in their trench coats and hats, these wounded angels who keep their righteousness and romanticism concealed, sometimes even from themselves. Chandler, justly famous for his similes and wisecracks, saw kisses in cocktails and the promise of sex in the first drink of the evening in a quiet bar. The twist is that the promise of sex always exceeds in pleasure any possible fulfillment. "Alcohol is like love," Terry Lennox says (and Marlowe agrees) in *The Long Goodbye*. "The first kiss is magic, the second is intimate, the third is routine. After that you take the girl's clothes off."

RECIPES

In Williamstown, Massachusetts, a bartender made gimlets with Triple Sec, Lillet, limes, and sugar instead of Rose's Lime Juice. It seemed to me a lot of effort to produce unspectacular results.

While I regard the Gibson as interchangeable with the martini except for the onion, I know of some who feel that the ratio of vermouth to gin is slightly higher in a proper Gibson.

If you set your next detective novel in Nice or Cannes, consider serving Negronis to your suspects. Some recipes call for one-third gin, one-third sweet vermouth, and one-third Campari. Dispensing with the vermouth, I use half gin and half Campari, garnish with a slice of orange, and toss in a lot of ice.

The next time I solve a murder I am going to confront the culprit at a garden party after he has recited a false narrative of events. With a dramatic flourish I shall lift my glass and say, "That story should be taken with as much salt as rims the glass of this margarita."

Yellowtail

STUART DYBEK

There are rare days in the Florida Keys, in summer between hurricane scares, when the wind wafts from nowhere and then not at all, and beneath the platinum tonnage of sun the sea flattens into the bluegreens that never fail to leave you young. Silhouettes of frigate birds, the only shade, glide an Atlantic becalmed to the horizon; on days like this people say you could row to Havana. Maybe the frigate bird overhead can see Cuba ninety miles away.

I'm seven miles out, free diving on the reef in dazzlingly clear aquamarine. Only a few such days, really, in summer, in a lifetime, when calmness and clarity turn the soul into a mirroring inner sea. It's a deceptive state of being, one that seems as ordinary in its naturalness as that gliding frigate bird or the leopard ray perfectly visible thirty feet below, also gliding. But the human animal outfitted with fins, mask, and snorkel swims in an extraordinary dimension where calmness and clarity are features of the ecstatic. Communion with the elemental—light, air, water—brings with it intimations of the eternal, and the eternal can make you reckless.

So when I see, perfectly visible fifty feet below, a startlingly large yellowtail snapper rising from a school too deep for me to dive to, I follow him out past the lighted tower that marks American Shoal.

I should mention that besides fins, mask, and snorkel, I'm wearing a thin wet suit, more to protect me from jellyfish than for warmth in the eighty-degree water, and a weight belt with eight pounds of lead to counter the wet suit's buoyancy. I'm also carrying a speargun. It's a Riffe gun made of teak. When I saw it on sale for four hundred dollars in the window of a dive shop, I hesitated even though the aluminum Dacor gun on which I'd relied for twenty-five years was corroding, until a friend said, "For Christ's sake, is there anything you like to do better? If you were a golfer you'd spend that and more on a set of irons." My first time in the water with the Riffe I couldn't cock the rubber slings that power it and for a humiliating few minutes wondered if I'd bought a gun I wasn't strong enough to load.

I should also mention that snappers are among the best eating of all fish and that my favorite of the snappers is the yellowtail. If I had to choose one out of the more than one hundred edible species of fish that come from Florida waters, it would be yellowtail snapper. I've seldom seen it in northern markets or on the menus of restaurants outside of Florida or the Caribbean. The flesh isn't quite as firm as that of most snappers and maybe it doesn't hold up in travel—yellowtail needs to be kept as well iced as oysters. My hunch is that it wouldn't travel much even if it traveled well, that the locals probably consume all that is caught. It's a trout-beautiful fish, sleeker in body than the other snappers, with an identifying zooty yellow stripe extending from forward of its eye to its deeply forked yellow tail. Above the stripe, an unbreakable yellow code dots and dashes a field of bluish scales; below, pink and shimmering white silver. As looks go, the juveniles schooling on inshore reefs hold their own with the generally gorgeous population of tropicals. Mature yellowtail, sometimes schooled so thick they make me think of the way Audubon described seeing flights of flamingos crowding the sky, cruise the offshore reefs. Only rarely have I speared one. They're wary and quick, and unless hit solidly their soft flesh will tear free of the spear. Better to line fish for them. A keeper is twelve inches, and usually they weigh from one to three pounds, though occasional larger fish called "flags" are caught at the drop-offs. The world record is eight pounds, nine ounces. The flag I'm following out in the direction of Cuba looks like a new world record.

I'm beyond the drop-off, in blue water, when I hear a voice, ghostly at first, like a bad connection on a telephone. It reminds me of times when as a child I'd hold my nose, close my eyes, and submerge myself in my Saturday-night bath. I'd hear voices traveling the pipes from the various flats of our apartment building. Though they spoke in different languages— Spanish, Polish, Czech, Filipino, broken English—I could translate what I heard into anger, laughter, secrets. The voice I hear now seems to be giving an impassioned speech. Gradually

I realize that, for my benefit, the speaker is speaking heavily accented English and that what he has to say is less about the sugarcane quota, the embargo, and the evils of capitalism than about the dialectic between fish and fruit. It's not that he's forgotten or allows me to forget that long ago the Kennedys took out a Mafia contract on him and that the CIA plotted to poison his wet suit or blow his head off with an exploding cigar, but that he also has a lifetime's experience to relate what an island people know about the way seafood takes to the banana, the mango, papaya, coconut, strawberry, guava. There are bridges in cooking, he explains, certain ingredients that connect tastes in the way that the word *like* connects images in a simile. *What connects fish and fruit?* he asks (all his questions are rhetorical). Onion. Onions, peppers, salt, and lime.

Speaking of cigars, I'm increasingly aware of the occasional whiff of cigar smoke I've been tasting through my snorkel. If not for a becalmed sea it might make me queasy. He's recalling how his comrade, Che, would get seasick when they'd go deep-sea fishing. He's reminiscing—actually, it's closer to bragging, about his own spearfishing expertise. Memories delivered like a piscatory manifesto: days when he was young, diving on the Bayo de Cochinos, the Bay of Pigs, long before the invasion. *Do you know they dropped napalm on Cuba before they dropped it on Vietnam?*—a question he asks without pause for an answer. That bay, he explains is named not for the pig, but for the *cochino*, in English, the queen triggerfish, a reef fish as spectacularly extravagant in design and color as angelfish.

Cochinos are found in abundance there. In the heat, how well they go with a simple salad of raw onion, chilled papaya, and pineapple dowsed in the juice of bitter oranges.

It's a fish I know, one that was a favorite on the island in the Caribbean where I once taught junior high. That was where I learned to spearfish. The cochino was called oldwife there, and when the fishermen tied their wooden boats to the dock and tossed up the day's catch, the local women would bid for oldwives.

He's speaking now of fresh dolphin, with its natural affinity for avocado, carambola, and fried plantains; of grouper, not the overfished, commercially caught groupers like the black with their large-flaked flesh, but smaller groupers such as the vividly speckled red hind with their tighter-grained, lighter flesh that takes so well to passion fruit and mango. He names fish that only fishermen and ichthyologists know: spadefish, porgies, palometa, and the beautiful hogfish. Although hogfish is sometimes called hog snapper, it is actually a large wrasse taken mostly by spearfishermen; its fine white flesh is so subtle that the fish goes wonderfully with a peach salsa. Most of the fish he's mentioned live on crustaceans and have a delicate flesh, but even the hogfish, he says, is not the equal of the yellowtail.

Why the yellowtail? he asks, rhetorically.

Because there are fish that can be eaten only if filleted or steaked or smoked or broiled or fried, but yellowtail snapper can be prepared in every way one can imagine—grilled, sautéed, poached, baked in parchment, steamed in a banana leaf, and paired with most any fruit. He's dictating a recipe for yellowtail in which the whole fish is scaled, scored, seasoned with garlic salt and pepper, and dipped in oil so hot that the gill flaps are almost crisp enough to eat. It can be done in a large cast-iron pan with a cover or even in a wok. What's crucial is searing heat that seals in the succulence—frying or broiling the whole fish is basically a passable substitute for grilling it over white-hot coals.

Snapper served whole is a favorite dish in many cultures. If the cuisine isn't Cuban then mostly it's made with a snapper other than yellowtail. The menu always claims it's red snapper, the fish most people recognize. In my old Chicago neighborhood, a barrio called Pilsen, one of my favorite restaurants, the Ostenaria Playa Azul, makes the classic *huachinango veracruzana*: slivered garlic is implanted under the scored skin and the fish is served to be wrapped in corn tortillas along with its dressing of cilantro, tomato, pepper, lime, and avocado. In Thai and Vietnamese restaurants, the fish is finished in *nam pla*, fish sauce, and some combination of spices and herbs that includes a licorice taste—basil, tarragon, star anise—as well as cilantro, ginger, coconut milk, lime. I improvise versions in which the fish is set on a bed of basmati rice swathed in a sauce that can have endless variations. For example: Pour into a blender coconut milk, add chopped fresh pineapple, ginger, a hint of garlic, a little scallion. After blending, the taste should be that of an interesting milk shake. Meanwhile, lightly sauté chopped onion, chopped fennel shoots (save the bulb for another dish), lemongrass, more ginger, hot pepper, curry powder, and cumin all to taste ("to taste" means don't overwhelm the fish) followed by the zest and juice of limes. Then stir in the mixture from the blender and heat gently. Adjust salt and pepper, add generous snippings of basil, cilantro, and scallion, and a sprinkling of peanuts. It's exquisite with snapper, flounder, or fresh dolphin, and can almost redeem a fish as bland as tilapia.

The voice underwater is talking about Guantánamo and an American imperialism in Cuba that goes back to 1898, but also about a combination of yellowtail, mango, saffron, and pink shrimp in a stock from their shells; about how canned guava juice can be puréed with ripe guava and ripe plantains that have been sautéed with nutmeg and paprika, then the sauce studded with strawberries. But the voice, growing fainter, is momentarily obliterated by the Navy jets from the base at Boca Chica burning thousands of dollars of oil overhead, a busted sound barrier roar of awe and terror as if an armada of two-stroke outboard engines that can grind a swimmer into bloody hamburger are bearing down, and the flag I've been following, which has stayed just out of range of my spear, dives, flashing his sunrise stripe, and I follow him down into the indigo-tinted seemingly bottomless Gulf Stream, deeper than I've ever dived before, where the voice is still barely audible, nearly imaginary, like the voices in the pipes in Pilsen long ago, more Spanish than English now, saying a litany: *anon, canestel, sapote, mamey, tamarino.* But among the names of fruit and fish are other names, Nixon, Reagan, Bush, and questions—rhetorical, about how such a great, rich democracy, free of dictators, lost its vision; how it came to be a mediocracy led by crooks and movie stars, by democratically elected warmongers. A last glint of a yellow tail, and the flag disappears into the depths and the voice fades out on "coconut water, regime change, *guanabana*, war criminals, flambé in rum. . . ." And then only my own heart beating for breath against my eardrums as I rise, looking up at the surface of the water as if it were a sky across which pass boatloads of starving Haitians crossing a perilous sea of plenty, and Cuban refugees fleeing a would-be workers' paradise, and drug dealers in cigarette boats fueled with coke and loaded with bales of square grouper, and an old man lugging a shark-mangled marlin, and the largely unregulated international factory ships long-lining the last mercury-contaminated swordfish and tuna. I surface beneath a lone frigate bird and the sun beats down on my confused politics, as without a fish to show, I start the long swim back.

Mezcal

MARK STATMAN

I.

Avenue of Mexican Dreams

I want to go back and
I will go back
are not the same thing
I can see trees through the window
and cars and buses
roll down 7th Avenue in Brooklyn
bad mufflers and shrill brakes
and I'm afraid every second
they'll wake Jesse too soon
from his morning nap

But here's the picture:
a dusty road, dry blue sky
and a mezcal place
where there's six kinds to choose from
I get to sample each one
before I decide
que le gusta
todos
everyone laughs
and one man asks me
if I'd like some *chapulines*
they're not exactly grasshoppers
dried and covered
with red chile and salt
he puts one in his mouth
what can I say?

—Mark Statman

II.

The first time I drank mezcal, fifteen, maybe sixteen years ago, I did it all wrong. Got it all wrong. Didn't get it at all. I was in Oaxaca, the orange-flower city in southern Mexico, staying in a hotel four blocks south of the Zocalo (the main town square), a few blocks east of the red light district. I knew that mezcal was a drink Oaxaca was known for and had some idea that it was something like tequila. But I wasn't sure how to try it or even how to buy it. I didn't realize at the time that you could walk into any supermarket in the city and get a bottle. It was my first time in the country and I was clinging to visions of the drink being somehow different and forbidden. I was sure I could get it in one of the many bars in the city, the men-only places with the swinging doors from which *rancheras* and mariachi echoed early and fights and drunks emerged late. But guidebooks routinely warned foreigners against these places and I wasn't exactly sure I was ready to defy the guides.

What I did, and this is what I mean about getting it all wrong, was that the first time I drank mezcal it was out of a souvenir. I was at a little shop near one of the main markets and hanging from the walls were small round jars, the San Bartolo de Coyotopec black earthenware that Oaxaca is famous for, the word *Oaxaca* painted in white across a red circle, red wax sealing the bottle's cork. I asked for two, overpaid, and took them back to my hotel.

But how to drink? There was a little plastic packet of salt, chile, and (I later found out) ground-up maguey worm. Like tequila? Salt on the wrist? Shot? Lime to finish? I went to a small *tienda* across the street, bought some limes. I used my Swiss Army knife corkscrew to open the mezcal. Salt. Mezcal. Lime. Awful. Awful, awful, awful. A taste like kerosene. Like turpentine. Paint thinner. Undrinkable things. I opened the other jar. Tried again. Practically choked. What was the deal?

Maybe you had to mix it. I had some Squirt, the likable lemon-lime Sprite of Mexico, except it's much fruitier and not as sweet. But the mezcal ruined the Squirt. And that was that. My mezcal experiment was over. Or so I thought.

A little less than a year later, I was back in Oaxaca again (I always want to be in Oaxaca again). I finally worked up the courage. I decided to walk through those swinging bar doors, to the places where real men go. Where women never go. Where gringos are warned to stay away. But I'm going to try it. I'll go in and have a beer, see what the fuss is all about. I'm a tourist, after all. I'm allowed to be stupid, right?

So I go in, feeling a lot less brave than when I'd imagined it all (John Wayne, Alan Ladd, Gary Cooper, me). The place is full, warm cigarette haze, talking, shouting, jukebox. I'm lucky, though, and find a table in a corner. I ask for a *cerveza, bien fria*, the way you're supposed to. A man at a table next to me turns and raises his shot glass in salute. I respond with my beer. No, no, no, señor, that won't do. He gets up, half walks, half stumbles to my table. He calls to a waiter, orders something. *Que es eso?* I ask, the shot glass delivered, slopping slightly. *Un tragito de mezcal, amigo.* A shot of mezcal, friend. And here's where the tourist appears. *Pues, como tomo este?* How do I drink this? My friend is astonished. He gestures. *Asi.* Salt on the wrist. The shot. The lime. *¡Andale!* He says. Go on.

I don't want to offend him. I don't want to offend anyone. I feel like every person in this bar is watching the pale-skinned idiot from the U.S. and all I want to do is get out of here. So, thinking the surest way to leave safely and with some kind of dignity is to follow instructions, I do. Salt. Shot. Lime.

And I'm in heaven. I've never had anything like it. A joyful warmth, mouth, throat, stomach. Smoke. Earth. Air. This stuff. I have another. Another. "I seem to see now, between mezcals," Malcolm Lowry writes in *Under the Volcano* (one of a very few novels that mentions the stuff), "this path, and beyond it, strange vistas, like visions of a new life." Newfound friends are buying shots for me. I'm buying shots for newfound friends. We drink. We toast. *A Mexico! A los Estados Unidos! A amistad y todo el mundo!* Finally, I stumble-walk back to my hotel, half-surprised at how sure I am of where I'm going. Light-footed. Wise. That night I sleep the sleep of the innocent and blessed. The next morning, I wake up clear-eyed, happy.

I had found real mezcal. And I found out from my friends how and where to buy it. Never in the black jars, those are for tourists. *Poison*, one man says, spitting on the floor of the bar. And, shrugs another, you can buy mezcal in the supermarkets, but those are only so-so. The real places to get mezcal (besides these bars, of course) are on the roads outside the city, where the mezcal is made. Except you shouldn't even buy the mezcal in the bottles they sell because those, while all right, are also not of the highest quality. They are mainly for tourists, albeit Mexican ones, usually from Mexico City, who, my friends claim, don't really know any better. Instead, I'm told, you bring your own bottle and ask them what they're selling that day, because there are many ways that mezcal is made.

So I head out of the city in my rented blue VW bug to one of these places, out route 175, the *Carretera Internacional*, heading east toward Mitla, past the Tula Tree (the oldest in the world), past the roads leading to the ruins at Yagul and Dainzu (where it's rumored you can hear the voices of the dead, sacrificed losers in the *juego de pelota*), and I come to a *fabrica de mezcal*. The main factory is out toward the back (there are tours for those who want to see the whole mashing/cooking/distillation process). In the front is a shop where the already-bottled mezcal is sold, colorful woven rugs (for sale) hanging from the walls. There's also a kind of bar here (not the swinging-door variety, though; this one is open to everyone), and it leads out to a shaded wrap-around-the-corner veranda, where you can sit, sip, relax, and look out at the plains, blue sky, and mountains. My bottle in hand, I walk up to the counter.

What would you like?

What do you have?

A lot. They show me sample bottles. One variety is gold, another clear. In one bottle sits a banana; in another, a large maguey leaf. One bottle has a long green chile pepper floating in it; in another there are chunks of pineapple. The fruits and vegetables have clearly been soaking for some time.

Que le gusta? I'm asked.

No sé. I'm not sure.

Out come tiny plastic shot glasses. Together, we try them all (the *chapulines*, too: little chile-covered, salted dried grasshoppers). We toast and drink. Delicious, we all agree. But which do I want? I decide on the gold. I'm not sure why. It's the first one I tried. It's the one I like the most. Who can say?

I give them my bottle. They fill it up. I pay, wave goodbye. *Nos vemos!* They know they'll be seeing me again. And year after year, with every return visit, my bottle in hand, happy refills.

III.

Mezcal refers to all varieties of *aguardiente* or hard liquor that are produced from the heart (or *piña*—it looks like a pineapple) of the agave or maguey plant. Tequila is one of these, but tequila specifically comes from the town of Tequila, near Guadalajara, and from the *agave tequiliana*. Because tequila is big business, most of it is not made for local consumption. While the quality of tequila can vary greatly, the basic production and the basic flavor of tequila remain very consistent.

The opposite is true of mezcal. Except for the horrible stuff contained in the pretty black jars of Oaxaca and the more commercial brands, most mezcal is pretty much meant to be drunk close to where it's made. For a variety of reasons, including soil conditions and weather (the maguey of Oaxaca, for example, prefers warmer, drier weather), mezcal flavors can vary from region to region, even from town to town. Adding fruit and chiles during the process will change the flavors even more. Unlike tequila, mezcal is rarely, if ever, mixed. Diana Kennedy, the goddess of Mexican cooking, recommends drinking it straight, with salt and lime if desired. Nancy Zaslavsky, in her cookbook/guidebook *A Cook's Tour of Mexico,* suggests a cocktail of mezcal, orange juice, and lime juice, recommended to her by the brothers Lopez, Jose and Fernando, the owners of Oro de Oaxaca, the best-known commercial mezcal.

Contrary to some myths (often perpetuated by some mezcal makers), mezcal was not given to the Indians by the gods (that may have been *pulque*, another taste entirely, made from the leaves only of the maguey). Rather, it was the conquering Spaniards who first started making mezcal as a way of paying (enslaving) the Indians they put to work in the mines. It's a sad and stupid part of the history of this otherwise wonderful drink.

The best and best-known mezcal comes from Oaxaca, and the best way to get it is, well, to go there and get it. But if a visit isn't in the cards, there are some pretty good mezcals available in the United States. Gusano Rojo and Monte Alban are the two best known. Each is golden, fairly tasty, though with a vaguely flat aftertaste that is typical of the industrially produced mezcals. Both come complete with a maguey worm (another tourist thing, to show that it's real mezcal) floating at the bottom.

But the champion of the imports is Encantada. The price is steep, usually twice that of Gusano Rojo and Monte Alban, but worth it. It's a clear mezcal and there's no worm. Just mezcal as good as it gets, subtle, soft, divine.

I've been trying for a long time to think about how to describe mezcal's flavor. It's hard, in part, because there are so many variations, so many possibilities for what that flavor can be. Good mezcal is something you practically breathe. It goes down smooth, light, smoky. It's all at once rich, earthy, and delicate. Although the salt and lime or the chiles, grasshoppers, and worms, if you like, are part of it, most times I don't even use those. I like to sip, to savor. When I do, I'm remembering Mexico, remembering Oaxaca:

> darkness framing the squareness of houses
> lavender lime and yellow under lights
> darkness framing the squares of faces
> and plazas
> trees gardens gates
> cornering the angles into life
> the sounds from a radio
> *quien como tu*
> the one two three
> of a burro and a man walking down
> the stone street
> amplified insect buzz
> of insects, cars and trucks
> going in and out away.

So pour a glass. Put on a Los Panchos CD (my favorite is *Epoca Romantica*). *Que rico. Que sabroso. ¡Andale!*

The Path of Righteousness

MATTHEW BATT

There are three schools of thought on contemporary bread. The first says that baking is *Fun and Easy!* and all you need is one of those handy-dandy Donco Magic Bread Machines and an index finger and you'll have fresh bread coming out of your shorts by morning. These people are not bakers. They are simply pressers of buttons and they are an abomination. The second school of bread-thought says that making bread is like getting in touch with the Great Baker of the Universe, who kneaded our souls from sweet, sweet bulgur wheat. These people are not so much bakers as baked. The third school says, *Baking is freaking hard.* It is not sexy. It is not fun. You will not get your own cooking show, not even a chef's coat. Baking exists somewhere between art, science, and alchemy, and unless you are willing to dedicate a significant portion of your life to it—let's say your days and your nights for starters—don't bother.

This is what you need to begin:

1. A pound of flour
2. A pound of seedless grapes
3. 16 fluid ounces of water

Crush the grapes. Stir. Wait two weeks.

Taste it. Smell it. Touch it. It should eventually take on the color and consistency of pancake batter, but it's okay initially if it seems like gym socks steeped in rancid milk. It's alive.

~~~~~~~~~~~~~~~~~~~~~~~~~~~

My friend's father used to make bread from scratch every week, and as a kid she loved to watch him knead the dough, the kitchen dusty and illuminated with flour. I didn't have such an easy orientation to fathers. My adoptive father is dead; my biological father is observing strict radio silence; and my grandfather—the only consistent father figure of my life—has been wallowing in woman trouble ever since my grandmother died. As for me, my wife and I are getting to that point in time when we either start trying to have a baby or get the pipes capped off. Instead of making a decision, I started to bake.

My wife, a tremendous collector of cookbooks, had a copy of *Nancy Silverton's Breads from the La Brea Bakery*. She said it was supposed to be the best, and, other than the author's inclusion of her own name in the title, it seemed like a decent book.

Silverton says that the only bread worth making is sourdough, and the only way you can make it is with a starter. It's as primitive as cooking gets. Once you have your starter—essentially a live bacteria culture that produces, among other things, carbon dioxide, alcohol, and yeast—all it takes for the rest of your baking days is flour and water.

I have a friend who has a starter that her great-great-great-grandfather began in nineteenth-century Austria. It's seen the invention of electricity, the eradication of American slavery, the rise of the internal combustion engine, and has survived almost more war and violence than any one nation can claim. It slept in sleeping bags to stay warm, hid in root cellars to keep cool—it's nearly two hundred years old and yet every day it is reborn.

To me this sounds better than children, better than parenthood. In this world, where little girls wear skimpy dresses and little boys are sprouting guns for hands, why would anybody want a child? What do I want a kid for when I can make bread older than Napoleon?

~~~~~~~~~~~~~~~~~~~~~~~~

A pound of flour. A pound of water. A pound of grapes. Wrap the grapes in cheesecloth. Mix the water and flour in a jar. Squeeze the grapes into the mixture. Keep it cool in the basement. Wait for two weeks while it gets its mighty funk on.

I visit the jar every day like a bootlegger, but I can't do anything until the fifth or sixth day, when things get really nasty.

By day seven the mix is clotted and greasy and resembles something you might find on an oncologist's specimen shelf.

"It's technically possible," Silverton says, "to make bread at this point." But who would technically eat it?

I watch a gassy bubble belch from the vat of oozing, oily starter and I remember where I'd heard the phrase "La Brea" before. The tar pits.

"The culture has already developed the activity it needs to make a loaf rise," Nancy says. Like gangrene, I think, or botulin. "But the bread you'd get wouldn't taste or look as good as it could."

~~~~~~~~~~~~~~~~~~~~~~~~~~~~

It's day ten and I have to remove the cheesecloth bag of grapes today. In the beginning, the bag tried to remain buoyant, optimistic. But by day three it gave up and sank. I open the lid and sulfurous fumes escape like evil spirits. As my eyes tear up, I wonder if these gases are flammable, if the water heater pilot light will ignite them and turn my house into a convertible.

I plunge my hand into the goop.

It feels as though I have just thrust it into a chilled, Vaselined glove. After groping around in the cool, slick contents, I grab the grapes. It is not a relief.

When I was a freshman in high school, our gym teacher, Coach Chuck Bova, took all the "men" into the gymnasium. He was a huge man who had muscles instead of hair. "When you guys are in the shower, pulling your puds like a bunch of homos," he said, "you need to be checking your balls for lumps." With that he threw a small sack at my friend Tim. Tim shrieked and tossed the bag to me.

My best guess is that it was a pair of squishy silicone orbs the size of—well, life-size. One of said orbs contained a "lump." The entire package was wrapped in a makeshift, panty-hose scrotum.

That is what those grapes felt like.

A couple of years ago my wife tried to get a sourdough starter going but ended up making a home-brew batch of penicillin. My mom couldn't make toast without the fire department knowing about it. My dad used Ho-Made white bread as hamburger buns. My grandmother could bake some resplendent cinnamon pastries out of the dough-waste from pies, but she grew up in Toledo during the Depression, when recipes were simpler, more opportunistic. *Put bone in boiling water, serve.*

By the time my mom was cooking for me, Cold War technology had taken over. If you couldn't microwave it, then what the hell good was it going to do you when the nukes flew and you were stuck hunkering in the fallout shelter for a hundred years? She can cook now, and I guess I can too, but I still don't know anybody who can bake.

Day fifteen. The prognosis is not good. Silverton insists we taste the starter.

I will not.

It seems to be a blend of beer, evil, and vomit rather than the key to artisan bread.

"Take care of your starter," Nancy swears, "and it will be ready to work whenever you are." I presume she means that for people like me, whenever will be never. I have to admit, however, I kind of like Nancy for her cruel abruptness. She is not afraid to tell me about failure. She is the Bobby Knight of baking. She is not an enabler. She is a disabler—a needler, a bully, a double-darer, a my-way-or-the-highwayer. The father I never had and am not particularly eager to become.

Maybe she's right. Maybe I should stick to buying Wonder Bread and babysitting other people's kids.

~~~~~~~~~~~~~~~~~~~~~~~~

Nancy's "Basic Country Loaf" recipe is sixty pages long. This includes the directions for the starter and a preamble about the baker's life, but still, sixty pages? This is the flour, this is the water, this is the oven—I get the idea, I think.

I like to read a recipe to get an idea of the proportions and the ingredients, and then close the book and make it myself. Nancy foiled this tendency. Her recipe is all micromanagement and brutish condescension. "Start here," she says, "and you won't have to unlearn any bad bread-making habits." And, by implication, those of you who think you know what you're doing, bend over.

"You should know that this isn't what most people would consider a beginner's bread," she says. "There's no commercial yeast to push the sourdough starter into action, so you've got to make sure the starter you grow is strong enough to do the work on its own." I interpret this to mean, *You'll be buying your bread again within a week.*

It's not that Nancy's a bad teacher, but I don't imagine any of her students have ever given her a Kiss the Baker! apron. Everything she says—and I don't yet know if she's right or wrong—undermines everything else I've ever done or known in the kitchen. I thought baking would be easy, intuitive, relaxing. She's stressing the science and the rigor and the pain and the failure and I just don't know if I can take it anymore.

"Know that the first loaf made with the new starter won't be as good as the fifth—just as you need to get used to handling dough, your starter needs to adjust to its surroundings." Don't give up too early, she begs. It's not *your* fault you're a failure.

I grew up Lutheran, so I can take a lot of unprovoked shame, but Nancy pushed me one step too far. "I don't mean to sound too much like your mom," she says, "but in cooking—and especially in baking—it's easier to clean up after yourself as you go." So what if she's right? So what if every time I put flour and water together I end up looking like a dough-covered Elephant Man? So what if I can't mix, or knead, or measure, or bake, or even clean up after myself without her telling me how to do it? The way she makes me weigh and measure and clean and fuss over everything like I'm running a fertility clinic . . . why doesn't she write in Sumerian or, better yet, just invent a new secret language that only priests, parents, and bakers can read?

But I don't have a choice. Am I not baking for my life?

~~~~~~~~~~~~~~~~~~~~~~~~~~~~

My first loaf sucks.

I went into it thinking, I'll do all the tedious proofing and resting and retarding and reproofing and wrapping and covering and dusting and fussing, and it'll be as inert as a bag of sand. Instead it's like I put a balloon on a tailpipe. It inflates so fast I can practically watch it blow up. And then when I slide it out of the proofing basket, it flattens like a sheet settling on a bed.

I bake it anyway and it comes out, more or less, like a dense, airless, Quonset-shaped loaf of despair.

~~~~~~~~~~~~~~~~~~~~~~~~~~~~

In Raymond Carver's story "A Small, Good Thing," a sadistic baker crank-calls the parents of a mortally injured son after they fail to pick up little Scotty's birthday cake. At the end of the story, the night Scotty has died, the parents confront the baker. But instead of bludgeoning him to death with his own rolling pin, the parents allow the old baker to ply them with cinnamon rolls until they're stupefied by all the gluten and sugar and they let him relate his own sad, sad story. Ends up, he's got no kid. Not even a dead one. And every night, all he can think about is being childless, repeating Sisyphean days "with ovens endlessly full and endlessly empty."

I wonder if Nancy is this lonely—if she bakes to make up for some primal loss. I don't know a thing about her, but I do know that baking is as difficult a thing as any needs to be. I need to figure out what it means to make something rise—to finish something that isn't easy or glamorous, but to breathe life into something nonetheless. But with that skill, that ability, comes responsibility. I am scared to death of becoming a father.

I do some research. I learn from Nancy's Web site, www.labre-abakery.com, that Nancy is no longer just Nancy but rather Nancy Silverton, Inc. I discover that La Brea bread is available here in Salt Lake City, approximately five hundred feet from my front door at an Albertson's grocery store—the one that smells like Old Spice and fried chicken.

To me—to Nancy, I am sure—this is not an entirely good thing. There's something tragic about the likelihood of Nancy in a pantsuit, trying to figure out how to make conference calls while illegal aliens bake bread and put her name on it.

I wonder if she can help me—if we can help each other. I wonder if, just maybe, I might get in touch with her and together we can puzzle through the problem of my falling loaves so I can feel less like Bob Dole doing a Viagra commercial and she can feel like a badass baker once again.

I call. She is not available.

I write, no response.

I click on the "Ask the Artisans" link. Nothing.

~~~~~~~~~~~~~~~~~~~~~~~~~~~~

Suddenly, Julia Child dies. I never knew her. I have never actually seen her shows, but I catch an old interview on NPR and I immediately go buy *Mastering the Art of French Cooking*. I put my sourdough starter in the refrigerator. I buy five pounds of beef bones and try to make a "nice brown sauce." This will make me feel better. This is what I'm *meant* to do, who I'm meant to be. Not some hair-shirted baker, but a saucier! Forget dour, sourdough Nancy—it's sweet, saucy Julia for me.

I roast the bones in the oven for hours. I reduce the stock for hours more. I'm making progress! I can see it! My wife, my friends—they'll *drool*!

I run to the store to get more bones and when I come back the house, the furniture, the pillows, the dog, the cat—everything—smells bloody.

I feel like a soiled, unfaithful, pathetic man.

~~~~~~~~~~~~~~~~~~~~~~~~~~~~

I've never met a real baker. I doubt many people have. They work the graveyard shift with the vampires and the hookers.

They work in fluorescent-lit, steam-injected, incubator-like rooms. They work alone with water, flour, yeast, and heat, and if anything is a fraction of a degree off, they fail. And if they succeed? The best they can really hope for is somebody biting into a slice of bread and saying, *Hm. That's nice.* People will get all pornographic about osso buco, but the best you can get out of them for bread is "nice." There are, accordingly, no celebrity bakers.

I found a recording of Nancy on, of all shows, Julia Child's *Cooking with Master Chefs*. Julia usually spent the program courting and cooing with her guest, but she didn't even appear on the show with Nancy. Julia's introduction is just a voice-over. Nancy had to bake alone. It didn't even look as if they left all the lights on for her. Sometime later, Julia finished the program by tearing apart the loaf of bread. She said it would go very nicely with soup. Or a salad. That's like saying your child would make a great pipe fitter. Or sandbag.

If you're a baker, you don't get to flambé your guests' eyebrows off or *BAM!* things into a sauté pan in front of a live studio audience. You don't get to swan around town to all the after-parties for restaurant industry studs, showing off your wounds and bragging about how many waiters you mowed down tonight. You've been asleep since the early afternoon so you can get up at midnight and be to work by one while the bars start to empty out and the couples neck in the backs of cabs and the radio is filled with love songs dedicated to everybody else but you.

~~~~~~~~~~~~~~~~~~~~~~~~~~~~~~~

In a surprisingly vulnerable moment, Nancy Silverton warns me not against failure, for once, but success. "If you're not careful," she says, "the bread can take over your life."

I think I am beginning to know what she's talking about. Everywhere I go, I look for other people's bread. I pick it up, break it apart, sniff it, look at the crumb structure, the density, the color, the aroma of the crust, the palate, the mouthfeel . . .

I eat it, too. Of course I eat it. But my capacity for enjoyment is limited. I will always be a Lutheran. I don't love to eat. Too much indulgence. Too much guilt. The greatest pleasure I get from my bread is that my fussy English cocker spaniel, Maggie, begs for it. And I mean *begs*. Plain, white, sourdough bread. She's a very, very good dog.

And yet there's something happening—something more than just baking going on. Over the course of the summer, I have gone through over three hundred pounds of flour and made at least ten loaves of bread a week. I learned how to add vital wheat gluten to help support my premature risers. I cut down the post-fridge proofing time so the loaves don't gorge themselves on the thin, warm air here. But despite all my little ministrations and incidental improvisations, I still have to feed my starter morning, noon, and night; a cup of water, a cup of flour. You can be the best baker in the world, but what it comes down to is that your bread is only as healthy as your starter.

My starter just turned one year old, but I still feel like every loaf is a miracle that rose in spite of me. What you put in the oven is not the same as what comes out of it. While it's in there, all you can do is chain-smoke until it's ready. You've got a thousand opportunities to fail. If you succeed, you'll be sure it's a fluke and that somebody will accuse you of trying to pass off store-bought bread as your own.

Nancy was right. The bread takes over. Just look at what I've done. I took a pile of flour, added some water, and now I've got a jar bubbling over with life. I don't even know what to do with myself anymore—I didn't exactly choose this, but there's no turning back now. I feel like there's somebody standing behind me, pushing me down a narrow, narrow path, barking, You've got bread to bake, mister! No more binge drinking or break dancing or anything anymore, because you've got your nighttime feeding to worry about, not to mention tomorrow's loaves to get ready, and if you don't start mixing by nine you'll be up till three and then you'll need to sleep half the day to get over it, but you can't because the bread's got to be brought up to room temperature before you bake, and then afterward you've got to let it cool before it's ready for the table or else it'll be all hot and colicky, and so you had better just get your act together, mister, because you started this mess in the first place, and whether you like it or not, pretty soon people are going to ask you to dinner, and they're going to say, *And why don't you bring that nice bread you bake?*, and then it's that birthday party next week, and then the faculty barbecue, and the Fourth of July picnic, and then all of a sudden they're going to ask to take your bread to that bake sale or the church festival or, Heaven help us, the school dance—even if you can't go—and how the hell do you think you could go? You've got your starter to take care of and sleep to catch up on and tomorrow's bread to begin tonight. Just what were you thinking? How the hell do you think this stuff works? Magic? Miracles? Modern marvels of technology?

It's bread, my friend. Just bread. Nothing could be simpler. Just ask any parent.

RECIPE

INGREDIENTS:

2 cups sourdough starter
2 cups warm water
5 cups flour, plus more
1 tablespoon salt

Take 2 cups of starter, 2 cups of fairly hot water, and mix it on low with 5 cups of good flour. It should be pretty wet. You'll add at least a cup more flour before you're done. You cannot always add more water. Mix it for 5 minutes in a standing mixer with a dough hook. Let it stand for 15 minutes. Add about a tablespoon of salt and mix again for another 4 or 5 minutes, this time adding enough flour, a quarter cup at a time, so the dough begins to ball and clear the walls of the bowl. Turn it out on a lightly floured surface for a few minutes—until it feels, as Nancy says, like a baby's bottom.

Put the dough in a big, lightly oiled bowl, and cover with plastic wrap for 3 hours. Turn it out once again, cut it in half, spank it on the counter to get the extra air bubbles out. Let it rest for another 15 minutes. Then, slide your fingers beneath the dough, palm up, so that you're vaguely shaping it into more of a ball again. Pick the balls up and place each into a lightly floured bowl—preferably something that breathes, like a colander or an actual willow proofing basket, but don't fret, any old bowl that's big enough to toss a salad will do. Tightly plastic wrap each bowl and place in the fridge for 8 to 10 hours. Unwrap the bowls, place a dishcloth or an old flour sack over the top of each bowl and let them warm up for a couple of hours—no more than three.

Heat your oven to 500 degrees, and put one of those square baking tiles on the lower-middle rack. If you've just got a pizza stone or a cookie sheet, it'll be fine; just take one bowl out of the fridge an hour ahead of the other one and then bake the loaves one at a time. Turn out the loaves on a nicely floured—and I mean a bunch of flour—pizza peel, or in a pinch the back of a cookie sheet will work. Cut an X or a C or whatever makes you happy into the top of the loaf with a super-sharp razor blade, slide it into the oven with a nice clean-and-jerk movement. Turn the temperature down immediately to 450 degrees, spray some water on the walls of the inside of the oven, and, quick, shut the door.

Take a breath. You've done just about everything you can do.

Have a glass of wine or three. Give it a good 40 to 50 minutes. Take the loaves out when they are the way they should be. You know how that is—the way you like them. Good and crusty, but airy and cloudlike inside. When you knock on the bottom of the loaf, you know it's done when it sounds to your dog like somebody's at the door. Let them cool down, and then give them to people you love. You've worked too hard to really enjoy them all by yourself.

The Green Fairy

ELISSA SCHAPPELL

The night sky was breathing, rising and falling in time with the sound of the ocean beating on the coastline below the rocky cliffs of Zambujeira do Mar. Bright glowing halos burned around each silver star. This ring-effect was what my husband, Rob, and I had been transfixed by at the bar in the center of the small fishing village, how all of the electric bulbs seemed to radiate golden auras. The edges of the tables, the bar, the faces of the other patrons, all seemed to be emanating light. It was like being inside a painting. Not just any painting—a van Gogh painting. It felt like you could see the hand of God in everything. Now, outside, the tops of the trees were as elongated as candle flames; the planets appeared as distant pinwheels. It *was* van Gogh's *Starry Night,* courtesy of the absinthe we'd drunk hours before in a little dive the locals frequented.

The absinthe was why we were crawling on our hands and knees up the steep dusty street to the cottage we'd rented for what we imagined would be six months, or perhaps a year.

We'd recently dropped out of our lives in New York City—abandoning the square world of publishing—to escape to the Alentejo region of Portugal, an impoverished area populated with cork trees and lemon groves. It was rumored that members of the RAF were hiding out on the farms that bordered our fishing village, which also rented out spartan rooms to artists and travelers. We'd come to write—not magazine or newspaper pieces—but novels and poems. Great Novels. Great Poems. We were intrigued by the somewhat adolescent theory espoused by the poet and *enfant terrible* Arthur Rimbaud (when he himself was hardly out of diapers) that to make truly visionary art one had to destroy any and all repressive attitudes that might prevent you from tapping deep into this fertile consciousness. For Rimbaud, imbibing absinthe was the blazing wrecking ball that indeed demolished his inhibitions and set fire to his brain. This made sense.

I wanted to have visions. I was prepared to behave badly. I wanted my life to burn with an intensity others would find blinding. I wanted to have the sort of adventures that would be the stuff of legend. I wanted my life to be romantic and decadent, and slightly, lightly, debauched.

As naive and ridiculous as it might seem, drinking absinthe seemed a good start. As Rimbaud said, "Knowing pilgrims, seek repose / By the emerald pillars of Absinthe."

Absinthe was *the* liquor of choice among bohemians, artists, and writers during the late nineteenth and early twentieth centuries. The Green Fairy played muse to such painters as Picasso and Manet, inspiring them to paint portraits of absinthe drinkers (Degas' drinker is a particularly marvelous study in degradation), but, more important, it literally influenced their vision, mixing dream-state with reality.

Some art historians attribute the birth of Cubism to Picasso and Braque painting under the influence. Van Gogh's work at Arles appears strongly affected by vision warped by regular infusions of absinthe. (One hopes that the pain of severing his ear to make a gift to a prostitute was somewhat diminished by the narcotizing effects of absinthe.) Toulouse-Lautrec carried a toot of the stuff in his hollow walking staff. His fondness for *la Fée Verte* (he painted posters glorifying her powers) rivaled his lust for cancan dancers.

The commingling of art and life as an absintheure is clear in the work of Oscar Wilde, as well as in the work of Charles Baudelaire, and that of Rimbaud's lover and dueling partner Paul Verlaine—who, despite denouncing absinthe on his deathbed, secreted bottles of it beneath his sheets.

In America the moribund Edgar Allan Poe regularly wrestled with the devil absinthe—and lost—while Ernest Hemingway became enamored with her in Spain, fortifying himself with absinthe before running with the bulls at Pamplona. Hemingway's opaline cocktail of choice was a Death in the Afternoon. As he writes in the voice of Jake Barnes in *The Sun Also Rises*, "The absinthe made everything seem better. I drank it without sugar in the dripping glass, and it was pleasantly bitter. . . . I poured the water directly into it and stirred it instead of letting it drip. Bill put in a lump of ice. I stirred the ice around with a spoon in the brownish, cloudy mixture. . . . I was very drunk. I was drunker than I ever remembered having been."

When absinthe was outlawed in America, Hemingway traveled to Europe to stock up.

Absinthe's proof hovers around 68 percent, which is commensurate with a quality vodka or gin. Its ingredients include star anise, anise seed, hyssop, angelica root, calamus root, fennel, coriander, licorice root, lemon balm, and dittany, but its essential ingredient is the neurotoxin thujone, which when taken in excess is lethal. It is thujone, distilled from the herb wormwood, that provides the hallucinatory effects. Its influence on the rods and cones creates a distortion, a fracturing of images and light. Wormwood (*Artemisia absinthium*) appears in the Bible a dozen times, including the Revelation of St. John: "And the third part of the waters became wormwood, and many men died of the waters because they became bitter." Wormwood is the plant that was said to be growing along the path *out* of the Garden of Eden.

The word *absinthe* is derived from the Greek *absinthion*, meaning "undrinkable." In Russian the word for absinthe is *chernobyl*.

I hadn't realized that absinthe was legal in Portugal, and wouldn't have known it had I not, our second week in town, had the good fortune to be in a bar where I spotted the dark green bottle. Its neck was wrapped in twinkly blue foil, the label proclaiming in Portuguese, "Absinto." At first I was sure I was mistaken.

I nudged Rob—he raised an eyebrow. He was in.

"Absinthe?" I asked the bar's owner.

It was.

"Are you sure you want to try?" she asked me politely. Very few American tourists loitered in this village, and thus many locals weren't sure what to make of us. We'd only discover later that the majority of the tourists, mostly German and Italian, had access to absinthe in Spain and Czechoslovakia and parts of Switzerland, and so they entertained little interest in it. Or perhaps they were just smarter.

"Absolutely," I'd said. After all, it was cocktail time. It was still light out—it wasn't as if I'd take a sip and go off, barking mad.

I'd seen the accoutrements of absinthe drinking in paintings. The glass swimming with the grass-green elixir, the cube of white sugar poised for destruction atop the silver slotted spoon, a flagon of water at the ready. Somewhat to my dismay the owner did not procure any of these but mixed a finger or so of emerald-colored absinthe with fresh-squeezed passion fruit juice. I was slightly disappointed, but still intrigued.

The green absinthe infused with the pulpy, reddish orange juice had turned the drink an unsavory, and rather distressing, murky brown. I brought it to my lips, my nose crinkling at the sharp licorice smell, and sipped. Despite the sour-sweet flavor of passion fruit, a bitter anisette with heady top notes of ethanol rode over my tongue, its finish not unlike that of a fine Robitussin. One sip should have been enough, and yet somehow it wasn't. Even as the fiery licorice flavor burned in the back of my throat, I took another taste, and then another. Feeling my muscles coming loose from the moorings of my joints, I began to feel languid and curious about what would come next.

After Rob and I finished our cocktails, we headed down to the cliffs where we often stood to watch the sunset. It was a lovely warm evening—the sky even more beautiful than usual—so we went down to the tide pools to gaze at the pink and pale orange anemones, iridescent limpets, and blue-black mussels. Gerard Manley Hopkins had been so enamored of sea anemones he'd worn one as a hat; pink and lavender with coral-tipped tentacles. Now wasn't that an absolute stroke of genius? Had I possessed at that moment the will to bend at the waist, I, too, would have been pleased to wear a sea anemone like a hat.

As the sky darkened, fading from a deep velvety violet into indigo, we clambered back up the rocks and returned to the bar.

There we each enjoyed two more absinthes, this time with only water. This cocktail was a spectral iridescent green. Lovely to look at, but without the fructose and clouding effect of juice, this drink even more closely resembled some sort of oblivion-inducing potion, an enticing poison. The taste was strongly alcoholic (imagine licorice-flavored lighter fluid), with none of the pretense of such gentle-on-the-palate anise-flavored aperitifs such as Pernod or Ricard. This was not an aperitif, not a drink to start the evening; this drink *was* the evening.

Hours later, as we crawled slowly and most happily toward our cottage, the sky hanging low over our heads like a tent, I imagined we were part of a parade of jeweled elephants, each holding the tip of the tail of the elephant in front of him in his mouth.

The next morning, fearing a crushing headache and a stomach knotted with pain, I awoke reluctantly, only to find, strangely, that I was not in the grips of any sort of conventional hangover. No, I felt as though I'd been struck in the spine by a delicate forked tongue of lightning. I had the strangest sensation that my left leg had, in the night, withered and gone numb. I sat up slowly, and, trying to get out of bed, realized I was unable to stand. After a few ballerina point-and-flexes, the feeling began to return and I was able to hobble to the loo. "Well," I thought, "I won't be doing that again."

For the rest of the day, I felt fine, though I had no energy at all. Certainly I had no brain to write—no burning visions lingered from the night before. I didn't feel possessed by the muse. Instead, Rob and I lolled on the beach as though anesthetized, intermittently taken by naps. Possessing neither the energy to walk to the water nor the strength to swim—the riptide created whirlpools that had drowned far stronger swimmers than I, even when my nervous system was tip-top—I opted to stand underneath a bracingly cold natural spring that crashed down the cliff side. By four o'clock I felt restored. As the cocktail hour loomed, I looked at Rob. It was decided.

By six we were drinking absinthe again, this time at a café. (Absinthe became so popular in Parisian cafés during the nineteenth century that the cocktail hour was christened *l'Heure Verte*, the Green Hour.)

This time eager to play barstool alchemist, we ordered our absinthe straight up with a water side. Deprived of the proper slotted spoon, we resorted to simply dropping the sugar cubes right into the bright verdant liquor and pouring in the cold water. With the first splash, the cloudy transformation from sparkling emerald into a jade opalescence began. The Portuguese call this effect "pigeoning;" the French, the very apt "louche."

We sat and savored our viridescent libation. The sugar helped enormously, accenting the inherent sweetness of the anise. It was bracing and medicinal, and divine. A powerful elixir. I had the sense that something big was about to happen.

An obsession was born.

We began imbibing every day. We would drink absinthe after a late-afternoon repast of petite sea snails steamed in their shells and eaten off a pin. Then we would go down to the ocean at sunset and watch the sky change from a piercing blue, to purple, to a dark and vibrating azure. We lay on our backs and watched the swifts diving from the cliffs and the cranes returning to their nests atop the atolls, their huge white bodies leaving contrails against a silky-looking backdrop of fiery rose and orange.

We stared into the tide pools. We talked about what work we were going to do the next day. I looked for a new hat. Later, we might continue drinking at our favorite watering hole, but most likely we'd go home and play cards with our friend, a painter who was likewise hooked, and listen to American music.

Our favorite absinthe was the locally made white absinthe, which came in a brown stone bottle with a ceramic stopper. Oftentimes the bottle had a famous image—Degas' ruined absinthe drinker, a sloe-eyed Lautrec showgirl—decoupaged on the front. This might have discouraged the casual cocktailer, but not us.

Under the influence of water this white absinthe became not a greeny opalescent but a shimmering white, milky and luminous as a deep-sea pearl. White absinthe elicited the strongest hallucinatory effects; it was the most narcotic, and the rarest. These earthenware bottles of *absinto blanco* became our grail. They were incredibly hard to find. Years later, we returned to Portugal to tour the Neto Costa absinthe distillery—the only sanctioned Portuguese producer of absinthe—and bought a case of green absinthe, but it was not the same. Tragically, after journeying all over Lisbon and out into the Portuguese countryside, chasing down leads on white absinthe bootleggers, we were left standing, quite alone, and quite without white absinthe, in the middle of a cow pasture.

~~~~~~~~~~~~~~~~~~~~~~~~~~~~~~

Once we had tasted white absinthe, we bought up every bottle we could find, traveling by bike to small towns nearby and then via a wreck of a rental car into Lisbon on our quest. No dive was too scary or possible lead too ridiculous to follow. We begged bottles from stores and restaurants—in one case the manager had to be convinced to go and get a ladder out of the basement in order to reach the highest shelf behind the bar, bringing down a pristine bottle furry with dust. We cajoled bartenders into selling us their half-drunk bottles.

Drinking white absinthe was sublime. I cannot compare it to anything I have ever had before or since, though I imagine distilled opium might come close. Over time I came to prefer my absinthe as I had had it the first time, with fresh passion fruit juice and a small handful of crushed ice.

I became addicted to the way the drink melted my bones and softened my muscles into uselessness, like an unseen hand traveling up my spine, massaging the cords in my neck, stretching out my legs. It made me want to recline on a fainting couch, though, save that, the beach, a chaise longue, or the top of a cliff would do. Drinking absinthe created the most desirous, languorous effect, and, unlike other alcohols, it did not cause me to become overly chatty or mean; it didn't make me weepy or encourage me to unburden myself on strangers. There would be no midnight confessions, no hurled tumblers, no slamming of doors, and no dancing on tables. There was only a delicious torpor. For a while.

It wasn't until nearly two months had passed that I began to understand what Oscar Wilde meant when he wrote, "After the first glass you see things as you wish they were. After the second, you see things as they are not. Finally you see things as they really are, and that is the most horrible thing in the world."

I started to see glowing rings of light during the day, and sometimes my eyes burned as though I had cataracts, but I couldn't look away from the sun. I could lie for hours unmoving, lost in the troughs of my thoughts, overcome, unable to speak. Sometimes I felt strange flutterings in my head, what felt like a moth trapped between my brain and my skull, but I didn't blame the absinthe. I sank deeply into a depression. I seemed unable to articulate my thoughts, and often imagined a large golden rope spinning in the sky over my head. Lying on the roof of our cottage, arms and legs out, I felt pinned to the earth. I couldn't imagine ever moving again.

Still, come cocktail time, I would drag myself upright and put on a dress and go out. I longed for absinthe. Draughts of beer didn't satisfy; wine tasted sour and flat. When we traveled to places where absinthe wasn't available—Paris, Pamplona—I missed it so much I packed a bottle, though we often killed this after only a day or two. It wasn't so much that I wanted the taste of it (though I do confess to an abiding fondness for bitter herbal elixirs such as Chartreuse)—I didn't even necessarily *want* to drink it, but I *needed* to. I was deep under the spell of the green fairy.

After another month I most certainly became unwell. I didn't care if we traveled—we never made it to Morocco. And during the day while my husband and a friend went out and rode their bikes along the coastline—coming back with great stories of towns with chapels that had the bones of saints in glass vitrines, a village with a raven chained in the main square—I stayed indoors. The most I did was walk along the cliffs, or go into town for lemons and cheese. Some days I sat torporously at my typewriter and stared into space. I read Jane Bowles and Virginia Woolf, and dreamed letters I never managed to write home.

I did not realize then that thujone can inspire seizures in people who have preexisting epileptic conditions. Anyway, although I'd had seizures as a child, I didn't consider myself epileptic. The few times throughout my life when I'd experienced olfactory hallucinations—a pleasant scent of oranges—I hadn't thought much of it, assuming everyone, occasionally, had those. Now, however, the neurological effects of the absinthe— the auras, the olfactory hallucinations (this time they were not sweet, but offensive: smoked meat, the smell of rotting pumpkins, human shit), the moments when I became "stuck," unable to move or speak for some period of time—coupled with depression, were conspiring to cause what would be a nervous breakdown I would not recover from for years.

~~~~~~~~~~~~~~~~~~~~~~~~~~~~

I didn't connect the absinthe drinking with the breakdown, but months later, after we returned home from Europe (our suitcase full of bottles of absinthe), it began to dawn on me. Educating myself about my type of epilepsy—temporal lobe—I discovered van Gogh was epileptic, and that absinthe exacerbated this disorder. *Sure,* I told myself, *blame the absinthe; what about the fact the guy snorted turpentine and ate paint?* Still, as much as I didn't want to admit it, it made some sense. The absinthe didn't cause the breakdown, but it didn't help it either. It ignited the spark. I didn't reveal this fact to anyone for a long time. Why should I? I wanted to drink absinthe, and I didn't want anyone—doctor, friend, or husband—suggesting I shouldn't.

Back home Rob and I learned to guard our stash jealously. Guests who poured themselves tumblers full of our *absinto* were not invited back. We shared only with a select few, slowly creating converts. A lovely result of this was that these new absinthistes would travel abroad and bring bottles back home for us. Since that time in Portugal, fourteen years ago, I have tasted many other varieties of absinthe—the Spanish and Czech varieties, and a few American knockoffs—but none compares to the hallucinatory effects achieved with the white bootleg absinthe we drank in Zambujeira do Mar, so many summers ago.

Even now, knowing I should not drink it, knowing it could cause me terrible harm, sometimes when I am given a new bottle, I take a taste. I'm holding out hope that perhaps I will discover an absinthe that brings about the same magical transformation I experienced for a short time that summer, but this time only for one night. Were I to be put in front of a firing squad, I would refuse the last meal, the cigarette, for one kiss of absinthe. Given a choice, I will take my absinthe in a glass of champagne, in part because the taste is divine, but also because the name—Death in the Afternoon—reminds me that it is best that I have just one.

If only to preserve my stash.

RECIPES

Death in the Afternoon

INGREDIENTS:

Veuve Clicquot, or whatever champagne you fancy
Absinthe

Hemingway gave the directions as thus: "Pour one jigger absinthe into a champagne glass. Add iced champagne until it attains the proper opalescent milkiness. Drink three to five of these slowly."

Momisette

The Momisette, which translates into "little mummy," was popular during the twenties, the era of the great archaeological digs in Egypt. This recipe calls for quite a bit of absinthe. You might adjust the recipe so as not to cause excessive damage to the nervous ganglia, and find yourself, upon waking, wrapped in bandages and semi-embalmed.

INGREDIENTS:

3 shots absinthe
½ shot orgeat (almond syrup)
Cold water
Ice cubes

Combine the absinthe and orgeat in an old-fashioned glass, then add ice and water to taste.

Persian Cuisine

SHUSHA GUPPY

It is a common belief among gastronomes that there are only two great cuisines in the world: French and Chinese. The more sophisticated and cosmopolitan, especially those who have traveled in the East, add a third: Ottoman, which covers a vast area east of the Danube, from Greece and the Balkans to the Middle East, and conjures images of succulent charcoal-grilled lamb and game, exotic stuffed vegetables, and elaborate sweets. Delectable national dishes—the Spanish paella, the English steak-and-kidney pudding, the Hungarian goulash—and regional specialties exist everywhere, but they seem to be variations on a theme. By contrast, a *cuisine* implies a wide range of dishes created and perfected by a people over centuries, and it has been a subject of speculation by historians as an expression of geographical identity and a criterion of sophistication. Western gourmets who have lived among Persians and tasted the best of their fare have always claimed that Persia too has an authentic and rich cuisine, of an artistic expressiveness on a par with Persian miniatures, rugs, and poetry, and certainly more delicate and varied than any exotic cooking west of China.

I am, of course, biased. My palate was formed by the best Persian cooking, and still prefers it to any other. Marooned on a desert island and long deprived of food and drink, I would not hanker for coq au vin or shepherd's pie with a pitcher of wine, but for a plate of saffron rice topped with eggplant and lamb *khoresht* (stew), and washed down with a glass of cool *doogh*—one part yogurt and three parts water, with a pinch of salt and a few sprigs of fresh or dried mint. Food is the agent of memory, and for me the opulence of colors, smells, shapes, and tastes of Persian cooking brings back the lost paradise of childhood. Long-forgotten events, occasions, and feelings leap forth from the past, conjured by the mention of a dish or the scent of a spice, and fill me with nostalgia for a *douceur de vivre,* which came to an end when I left home for Europe and was irretrievably lost after the revolution of 1979, the death of my parents, and the dispersion of our family. My *petites madeleines* are the aromas of certain herbs and condiments—saffron, turmeric, nutmeg, fenugreek, coriander—that, together with the smell of boiling rice, pervade the air of a Persian kitchen.

~~~~~~~~~~~~~~~~~~~~~~~~~~~~~

The origins of Persian cuisine go back to Persia's ancient history, to the Assyrians and Achaemenian empires (eighth to fifth century BC). In old chronicles it is reported that Assyrian King Ashurnasirpal II boasted of giving a "ten day feast, for 47,074 people," for which thousands of calves, sheep, lambs, ducks, geese, doves, stags, and gazelles, plus tons of fruit, vegetables, nuts, and cheese had been used. At the time of the Achaemenian Cyrus the Great (reigned 559–525 BC) and his successors Darius and Xerxes, when the Persian Empire stretched from the Mediterranean to the Indus, the cuisine was influenced by the variety of regional cooking. But it was under the Sassanians (third to seventh century AD) that the cuisine reached its zenith, and a culture evolved that combined gastronomy with social intercourse; table etiquette and talk were elaborated, and even the conduct of drinking bouts was defined. Many specialties, such as stuffed vine leaves—*dolmeh*—kebabs, and marinades were invented. When the Arabs conquered Persia in the seventh century and the country gradually converted to Islam, Persian cuisine and table manners were passed on to the Arabs. According to Firdowsi, the tenth-century epic poet, the nomadic Arabs were uncouth men who "fed on camel's milk and ate lizards," and who gradually learned from the conquered people their *adab*—gracious manners—and their refined cuisine. Contempt is the weapon of the vanquished, and disparaging references to the Arabs as the "lizard eaters" appear even in the works of Arab poets of Persian origin, such as the great Abu Nuwas (762–813 AD). Yet by the time of Haroon al-Rashid, who ruled the vast Islamic empire from his capital of Baghdad, the Arab table was famous for its lavishness and variety. It is recounted that one night, at the end of the eighth century, Haroon al-Rashid was invited to a gastronomic feast by his brother Prince Ibrahim. Amid the colorful array of aromatic dishes that covered the huge *sofreh* (a white tablecloth spread on the floor around which the guests are seated, leaning against bolsters and cushions, in strict hierarchical order in relation to the prince or the guest of honor; tables and chairs are recent imports from the West) was the most delectable concoction in the shape of a fish. Haroon asked his brother what it was and learned that it consisted of eight hundred tiny tongues of a rare river fish. "How much does it cost?" inquired the caliph. "One thousand dirhams," his brother replied with pride (about a thousand pounds). Far from being gratified at his brother's extravagance in his honor, Haroon was appalled. He ordered Prince Ibrahim to distribute the same amount of money to the poor, and as a further punishment forced him to give the container of solid gold in which the dish was served to the first passerby in the street.

This story, which sounds like a morality tale from *One Thousand and One Nights,* illustrates how the art of cooking developed and spread from Persia to the rest of the Middle East during the reign of the Abbasids (eighth to thirteenth century AD), whose court and administration were run by Persians. During their rule, the Persians cultivated and disseminated to the rest of the world pistachio, walnut, and almond; pomegranate, quince, and cucumber; peas and broad beans; saffron, fenugreek, coriander, and sesame; and much besides. I used to think that these claims were expressions of national pride, to be taken with a grain of salt, but recent historical studies have corroborated them (see the *Oxford Companion to Food* by Alan Davidson, Oxford University Press). Using these new ingredients, Persian cooking developed in variety and refinement, and the Europeans who traveled in Persia in the eighteenth and nineteenth centuries spoke of a cuisine on a par with those of France and China. Later, the Moguls of India, whose luxurious court and language was Persian, adapted it to local conditions and products. Even today many items on the menu in Indian restaurants indicate their Persian origin, although they are much more spicy.

In the past the only way for a Westerner to sample authentic Persian food was to secure an invitation to the home of Iranian friends. This was partly because certain ingredients—such as pomegranate paste, powdered lime, sour grape juice, rose water, barberries, and others—could not be found in the West, and partly because some dishes required long and elaborate preparations incompatible with the hurried pace of modern life. An entire day could be spent pounding ingredients with pestle and mortar, or sorting out, cleaning, and finely chopping mounds of herbs, preparing *advieh* (a special mixture of spices), and fruit and nuts. I remember walking to school in the morning and hearing the contrapuntal rhythmic sounds of pestle and mortar from houses, as if communicating secret promises of culinary delights. To cook *fessenjan* (literally, "the food of life") for a household of twelve, a great quantity of dried walnuts had to be shelled and pounded to pulp, which took hours. I can still see the heavy pestle and mortar in the corner of our kitchen—it required three people to shift it—the bowl carved from a single stone, the cook (our old nanny, who had become the cook after we left her charge) lifting the solid wooden club with both hands and bringing it down with a thud, over and over again, as if in a religious ritual, oblivious to my mesmerized presence.

Today, thanks to modern transport, shops and supermarkets everywhere overflow with fruits and vegetables from all over the world throughout the year. But in the Persia of my childhood the menu followed the rhythm of the seasons. The abundance of vegetables and herbs in the summer led to a greater variety of *khoresht*, while in winter pulses (dried legumes) and dried ingredients were used in different *ash* (thick soup). There were no freezers or refrigerators, only a cool larder where sacks of dry stuff—rice, flour, pulses—and jars of preserves, jams, pickles, and condiments were kept. In spring, hawkers came from the surrounding countryside with baskets of wild herbs they had collected in the woods and sold them to households—wild garlic, marjoram, spring onions, and chives. The special rice dishes, stews, and soups made with these were more aromatic and tasty than usual. In summer, crates of apricots, cherries, and plums arrived from the market and were consumed fresh or turned into jam and sherbet (fruit juice boiled with sugar as a basis for soft drinks), and I remember a camel bringing a load of melons and watermelons of all sizes to be stored and consumed daily. There was a great deal of activity toward the end of summer to make provisions for the winter: everybody lent a hand to sort out and clean tons of herbs—chives, parsley, mint, tarragon, and coriander—which were washed and spread on a cloth to dry in the sun. From high ground, the flat roofs of the village, covered with drying herbs, berries, and fruit, were a colorful patchwork.

Nowadays there are Iranian and Middle Eastern shops in the West where you can buy packets of dried herbs, spices, berries, jars of preserves, and other recherché ingredients, such as dried lime and sour grapes, to concoct a Persian meal in a fraction of the time it took in the past.

The food in our house was famous; my mother had a reputation as a great cook. Yet I do not recall ever seeing her busy in the kitchen, though she trained the cooks and supervised the cooking on special occasions. Only at *Norooz* (Persian New Year, on March 21, the spring equinox), did she make all the sweets herself—sweetmeats and baklavas, sugar almonds and marzipan fruits and other delicacies. The dough for the pastries was made variously with flour, rice powder, or powdered chickpeas and rolled out; we all helped, pressing tiny molds in the shapes of flowers and leaves and moon and stars. Her patience and tact in managing her relationship with the primitive and temperamental charcoal stove was a model of diplomacy, but the result was as lovely to behold as to taste. The tiny cakes were stored in tight tins pending the arrival of the New Year and the deluge of guests.

Some anthropologists believe that the elaboration of Persian cuisine was the by-product of women's social conditions: patrician women, being homebound, had nothing to do all day except prepare elaborate food for their large families and friends. It is a fact that in the country and among nomadic tribes, where women work in the fields and tend to the flocks, cooking is simpler and less varied. But this is true everywhere in the world. I tend to believe that the art of Persian cuisine is related to the cult of friendship in Persia and the Islamic tradition of hospitality throughout the Middle East. "A guest is a gift of God," goes the saying, and even the poorest Iranians regard it a matter of honor, *aberou*, to give hospitality with whatever is at hand. "It isn't worthy of you, but here is some bread and cheese," they say, even when they are putting a marvelous tray of food before you. "That which I admir'd very much in the way of Living of the Persians, beside their sobriety, is their Hospitality: When they Eat, far from shutting the Door, they give to every one about them, who happens to come at that time, and often times to the Servants who hold the Horse at the gate," wrote Sir John Chardin in his *Travels in Persia* (1673–1677).

Persian cooking lends itself to sharing: a dish of rice and stew for six can easily be stretched to feed eight or ten if supplemented with bread. And the presentation of food has always been important, as evidenced in old miniatures: the variety of colors and shapes creates a feast for the eyes as well as the palate, enhanced by music and song, as a setting for conviviality or a prelude to love.

~~~~~~~~~~~~~~~~~~~~~~~

Furthermore, like all traditional cooking, Persian cuisine is based on health. Food elements are divided into two categories, *garmy* and *sardy*—hot and cold—which have nothing to do with the food's temperature but with its properties. These correspond to the Chinese notions of yin and yang, or, roughly, vitamins B and C. The healthy diet is one that balances the two elements. The knowledge of the "hot and cold" nature of edible things was passed down from generation to generation, and you learned about it as you grew up. For example, chocolate—a good source of vitamin B—is very "hot," and you balance it by drinking fresh orange juice or *doogh*, which are both "cold."

When I was a child there was no penicillin, and our colds and flus were treated with quantities of lemon juice mixed with hot water and honey, herbal infusions at regular intervals to combat infection and bring down temperature, and chicken or meat broth to build up resistance. Too much "hot" food makes you prone to infection and fever, while an excess of "cold" elements gives you indigestion and nausea. You learned to recognize the symptoms: red, dry lips indicated *garmy* (hot); tummy ache and a watery mouth meant *sardy* (cold). A drink of *doogh* or fresh lemonade for the former, a lump of *nabat* (crystallized or rock sugar) for the latter were the usual remedies. I brought up my own children by the same principles, avoiding antibiotics as much as possible, and they seldom missed school on account of illness.

~~~~~~~~~~~~~~~~~~~~

"A cook is as good as her mistress," my mother used to say. For that reason even women who were not likely ever to touch a pot learned to cook, and handed down their skills to their daughters. Leaving home in my teens, I did not have the chance to learn. There followed years of student canteens and

Left Bank cafés in Paris. When I married an Englishman and settled in London, a friend gave me a copy of the *Larousse Gastronomique* as a wedding present, which, as its name implies, is an encyclopedia of European cooking; together with Elizabeth David's classics, *French Country Cooking* and *Italian Food*, it is still my main reference book for Western cuisines. But I soon discovered that my guests quite reasonably expected Persian food from me, and I began to experiment from memory, asking for the ingredients from Persia. Later, whenever I was at home with my parents in Tehran, I would go into the kitchen and watch the cook, jotting down her basic recipes in a notebook, without any exact measurements—my taste buds remembered and guided me. "You cook by eye," I was told, and indeed Persian cooking allows a wide margin of improvisation: the relative quantities or ingredients, the consistency of the sauces, the seasoning can all vary according to the taste and circumstance, as long as you keep to the basic framework. (In this respect Persian cooking is akin to Persian music, which is modal and also allows improvisation within strict rules.) Many of the dishes have a sweet-and-sour taste, quite different from the Chinese variety, the blend being so delicate that it is impossible to detect either sweetness or sourness, only a new taste. No two cooks can produce exactly the same dish—they say of a cook "her/his hand is tasty," or the opposite, even though the same recipe has been followed. I have found that certain Persian dishes are more popular with Westerners than others. The following recipes are among them.

ESSENTIAL PERSIAN COOKBOOKS

Najmieh Batmanglij's excellent and beautifully produced *Food for Life* and *A Taste of Persia: An Introduction to Persian Cooking* are very user-friendly, and, illustrated with examples from Persian poetry and art, plunge you into the atmosphere of a traditional home. I use them constantly and find the results vindicated by memory. Published by Mage Publishers, Washington DC.

Margaret Sheyda's *The Legendary Cuisine of Persia*, which won the 1993 Glenfiddich Award for Best Food and Drink Book of the Year, is also excellent, detailed, and accurate, with a great range and variety. Published by Lieuse Publications, Oxfordshire, England.

Entertaining the Persian Way, by Sherin Simmons, a Zoroastrian from Yazd, central Iran; it has scrumptious regional recipes in addition to national ones. Published by Leonard Books, Luton, England.

RECIPES

Rice

The Persian way of cooking rice is unique, as is the variety of rice dishes. Plain rice, served with various stews (*khoresht*) or kebabs is called *chelo*, or *polo*, while rice mixed with other ingredients is always called *polo*.

Chelo, Plain Rice

INGREDIENTS:

1 pound (2 cups) basmati long grain rice
4 tablespoons salt
8 pints water
3–4 ounces butter, or 3 fluid ounces cooking oil
½ teaspoon Persian saffron, powdered and dissolved in
    1 tablespoon hot water, with ½ teaspoon of sugar
    (optional) for garnishing

Rinse the rice in plenty of cold water four times. Soak it in 4 pints of water with 2 tablespoons of salt and leave for a couple of hours, if possible, then drain and rinse. In a large nonstick pot bring 4 pints of water to a boil; then add the rice and 2 tablespoons of salt. Cook for a few minutes, until the rice is half-cooked, stirring only once or twice to loosen the grains without breaking them. You'll know it is done when the grains lengthen and are soft on the outside but hard in the center if you press one between your fingers or bite it—usually 2 to 3 minutes for basmati. (Be careful: if overcooked, the rice becomes squashy. What makes Persian rice unique is that the grains are separate, light, yet perfectly cooked. Test after 2 minutes; it might be just right.) Drain in a sieve or meshed strainer—the water must run out immediately—and run a little cold water over it; this gets rid of excess salt if need be and makes the rice fluffy.

Rinse the nonstick pot and put it back on the fire, add the oil or butter, and the same quantity of water—3 to 4 fluid ounces. When melted, divide the mixture into two halves; leave one in the pot and keep the other on the side. The bottom of the pot must be covered with the oil and water mixture. Add ½ teaspoon of the liquid saffron and 2 teaspoons of the yogurt (optional), and mix.

Scoop the rice with a large spatula into the pot in the shape of a dome, cover, and let it cook 5 to 8 minutes on medium heat. Lift lid and pour the other half of the oil and water mixture all over the rice. Wrap the lid in a clean dishcloth and cover the pot tightly to prevent the steam from escaping. Leave on medium heat for another 5 to 10 minutes, then on low heat for another 30 to 40 minutes. Before serving, switch off the heat and leave the pot for 5 minutes so that the caramelized bottom—*tah-dig*—

literally, "bottom-of-pot," a delicacy—comes off easily. Take a few tablespoonsful from the top of the rice and mix the saffron liquid in it, so that the grains become reddish and gold. Carefully spoon out the rest of the rice on a platter, spreading the saffron rice on top. Break the *tah-dig* into pieces and arrange them either around the rice platter or on a separate plate. Serve with whatever *khoresht* you have prepared.

Kateh

This is a quicker and easier way of cooking rice, which I use for family cooking, leaving the more elaborate *chelo* for guests.

INGREDIENTS:

1 pound (2 cups) ordinary white long grain rice—
   not processed brands such as Uncle Ben's
2 teaspoons salt
3 ounces butter or oil, less if you are on a diet
3 cups water

Rinse rice well. Melt the butter in a nonstick pot. Add washed rice and salt and stir gently until hot (but not fried). Add the water and bring to a boil. Cover tightly and lower the heat to minimum—the rice cooks in its steam. Leave for 20 minutes or longer, then proceed as for *chelo* to serve.

Khoresht Bademjan (Eggplant and Lamb Stew)

INGREDIENTS:

3 to 4 eggplants, peeled and cut lengthwise, ½ inch thick
1 teaspoon salt (or to taste)
4 ounces oil
1 large or 2 medium onions, finely chopped
1 teaspoon turmeric
½ teaspoon black pepper
2 pounds boneless lamb or veal or beef or chicken (best
    braising or goulash meat, leg of lamb or veal), cut in
    1 ½-inch cubes.
2 to 3 cups water
3 tablespoons tomato purée
1 large tomato, skinned, peeled, and finely chopped
1 tablespoon powdered lime or 3 whole dry limes, *limou
    omani*, or 1 cup *gooreh* (sour grapes)
1 teaspoon *advieh* (mixed spices for stews)

Peel and cut the eggplants lengthwise in ½-inch slices,
sprinkle with salt and let sit for 15 minutes. Wash with
cold water and gently pat the slices dry with a tea towel.
Fry the eggplant slices in oil—it absorbs quite a lot—and
set aside.

In a pot, fry the onions until golden, add the turmeric,
salt, pepper, and meat cubes, and stir until brown. Add the

water, the tomato paste, the finely chopped tomato, and the lime powder or *gooreh*, and mix. Taste the seasoning. Let the meat simmer, covered, for about 45 minutes, or until almost cooked. Then mix in the *advieh*, and arrange the eggplant slices gently on the meat, basting them with the juice. Cover and let simmer for another 15 to 20 minutes. The juice should be creamy, so simmer uncovered if there is too much liquid.

To serve: arrange the slices around the serving dish and put the meat in the middle. You can use zucchini instead of eggplant, following exactly the same recipe. Another alternative is *qaymeh bademjan*: cut the meat in smaller, ¼-inch pieces; cook ¼ cup split peas until tender, and mix them with the meat before adding the eggplant slices. This is a very popular, delicious, and economical dish, as a pound of meat with ¼ cup split peas and the sauce become a large quantity of delicious stew. Serve with *chelo*.

Khoresht Fessenjan
(Walnut and Pomegranate Stew)

INGREDIENTS:

1 duck or chicken (about 4 to 5 pounds), cut up
2 medium onions
4 tablespoons oil

8 ounces dry walnuts, thoroughly ground in a food
    processor
1 pint water
1 teaspoon salt
¼ teaspoon pepper
Juice of ½ lemon or one orange
5 tablespoons pomegranate paste
½ teaspoon nutmeg
½ teaspoon cinnamon
1 clove garlic, crushed (optional)
3 to 4 tablespoons sugar
¼ teaspoon of saffron powder dissolved in 1 tablespoon
    hot water

Finely chop 1 onion and fry in oil until golden. Add the ground walnuts and stir continuously for about 2 to 3 minutes. Add 1 pint of water, salt, and pepper. Mix lemon or orange juice, pomegranate paste, nutmeg, cinnamon, and saffron (and crushed garlic, if you choose) and add the mixture to the walnut sauce; cover and let simmer gently on low heat for 30 minutes, stirring from time to time to prevent sticking.

Chop and fry the second onion in oil, add the duck or chicken pieces and fry for a few minutes. Cover and simmer on the lowest heat in its own juice for 30 minutes (1 hour if you use duck). Stir from time to time and add a tablespoon of water if needed. Take off the skin and the carcass bones from the poultry (not from drumsticks or wings), and add the pieces to the walnut sauce. Taste to adjust seasoning, adding a little sugar if needed. It should taste pleasantly sweet and sour. Cover and simmer for a further 30 minutes. Serve with *chelo*.

I often cook this sauce with meatballs instead of poultry, especially when there is another poultry item on the menu.

Meatballs

INGREDIENTS:

1 pound ground lamb, veal, or beef
1 large onion
1 teaspoon turmeric
Salt and pepper to taste

Grind the onion in the food processor and knead it together with the meat and other ingredients. Make balls the size of large hazelnuts, fry them in a little oil (or spread them in a shallow ovenproof dish and put them in the oven on medium heat for 15 to 20 minutes, shaking them a couple of times), and add to the sauce instead of the poultry.

Baglava (Baklava)

Homemade Persian baklava is quite different from what is usually served in Greek and Turkish restaurants. It is less gluey, smaller, and more refined.

INGREDIENTS:

7 ounces finely ground pistachios
7 ounces finely ground almonds
1 teaspoon ground cardamom
7 ounces granulated white sugar
3 ounces or about 8 large sheets phyllo pastry

For the syrup:
7 ounces white sugar
3 or 4 fluid ounces water
3 tablespoons Persian rose water (not the industrial
    variety available at pharmacies)
2 tablespoons finely chopped pistachios, for garnishing

Use a food processor to grind the pistachios and almonds thoroughly. Mix the ground nuts with carda-mom powder and sugar. Brush a shallow baking dish with warm melted butter. Line the dish with one layer of phyllo pastry, brush it with butter, add a second layer, and butter that as well. Spread 3 to 4 tablespoons of the nut mixture over it and press gently down to make it even. Cover with another layer of phyllo pastry, brush with butter, and spread some more of the nut mixture. Repeat until mixture is finished—about three or four times—and finish off with 2 layers of phyllo, each brushed with melted butter. Prick a few holes in the top layer of pastry, and put the dish in a 350-degree oven. Bake for 20 to 30 minutes, until golden. Meanwhile, prepare the syrup. Put sugar and water on medium heat and boil for 12 to 20 minutes to 220 degrees, until syrupy. Take the baklava out of the oven and with a sharp knife cut it into 1-inch diamond-shaped pieces. Pour the warm syrup over it. Sprinkle the chopped pistachios on top. When cool, gently lift the pieces out of the baking tray and arrange them on a plate.

All of the ingredients used in the above recipes are available in neat packets from Middle Eastern and Persian shops in the United States.

My Life with Sukiyaki

ANTHONY SWOFFORD

The first meal I ate at the Murai family home in Tokyo lasted twelve hours. When I arrived at 11:30 AM, Father Murai offered me a Kirin. He poured. In Japan it's essential that others pour your alcoholic beverages. At noon he started pouring sake, and the first course landed at the table, a plate of *gyoza*—a dozen plump half-moons of wrapper filled with a secret pork and ginger concoction, fried lightly. That the gyoza came from an ex-girlfriend's mother was for me both soothing and disturbing, a Proustian bite that forced me to recall one of the greater failures in my love life. But the gyoza wouldn't be the only Proustian memory-assemblers during this meal.

S and I met in college. I saved her from evangelicals. She'd first come to Sacramento in high school and had spent a semester with a friendly family of devout evangelical Christians who fed her American burgers and fries and fire and brimstone in equally high doses. In three months she gained ten pounds and a shockingly keen ability to experience Christian guilt, shame, and moral superiority—this from a girl who'd never seen a Bible before setting foot in America. After her high school semester in California she returned to Tokyo and took up the deviant life that any eighteen-year-old cherishes—beers with friends and sex with boyfriends, and rock 'n' roll and karaoke. She spent a few uneventful years in college in Tokyo and then she broke out for Sacramento and lived with the evangelical family while attending a local university.

That's when S and I met through a mutual friend, Mayumi, my Japanese-language tutor. The love S and I felt was instantaneous and brilliant, a flash of light on a cold February Sacramento day. We walked through the rose garden at McKinley Park, the bushes bare and brown and showing no signs of life, for the casual observer. But with S's hand in mine the bushes bloomed red and yellow, and I saw all their beautiful colors and smelled their scent. I said to myself that one day S and I would marry in this rose garden. I'd known her for about fifteen minutes. Three weeks later she left the evangelicals. They called her a sinner, and she agreed. We liked our sins.

At the time, I was putting myself through college working the swing shift at a grocery warehouse, 5:00 PM to 1:30 AM. My lunch hour was from 10:00 to 10:30. Two or three nights a week S drove from downtown Sacramento to the industrial and port area of West Sacramento and brought me dinner. The gyoza from her mother were a staple for me; she overnighted the filling to S every few weeks, a ten-pound frozen ball of goodness wrapped with dry ice and aluminum foil.

We'd sit in S's Mazda, badly dented from her five fender benders during one unfortunate three-week period. I'd eat six gyoza and a bowl of white rice and some pickles, perhaps a seaweed or cucumber salad. Most of the guys in the parking lot during the meal break were drinking from flasks, smoking weed, snorting speed, masturbating, or staring dumbly at the goddamn warehouse where we all spent eight hours a night at the boring, repetitive task of stacking yogurt and orange juice and raw meat on pallets destined for local grocery stores. During this bleak period of working labor in my twenties the only thing that ever gave me any hope and joy was my relationship with S.

Now, in the Murai home, I tasted S's mother's gyoza (they'd been delivered from her father's local food shop) for the first time in seven years. Sachiyo Murai had attended an all-girls high school with S and now the Murai family was hosting me for a few dinners during my research trip for a novel set in Tokyo. I knew Sachiyo exclusively through S's photos and anecdotes from high school: on the softball team they were a pretty pair of benchwarmers; at the New Year holiday Sachiyo worked long hours in S's father's shop, rolling gyoza, frying tempura, flirting with boys.

The gyoza didn't taste of Tokyo, though, they tasted of Sacramento and my love for a woman I'd abandoned when my older brother died of cancer in February of 1998. I was inconsolable, and in classic male fashion, I allowed my brother's death to color my entire life with darkness. My brother had died and I had to take others down as well, my beautiful lover one of those others who needed to go. What a fool. The gods of tragedy love men like me. We make their jobs easy.

There were nine of us at table: Sachiyo's mother and father, her older sister and her husband and their two daughters, her younger sister, and Sachiyo and me. Actually, for the most part, eight of us were at table because Mother Murai spent the majority of her time in the kitchen. It was a small kitchen in a modest and simple house, a house made to function as the center court for a family, with very little room or worry for decoration or empty space.

The kitchen consisted of a refrigerator half the size of your standard Sub-Zero. The two sinks were too small to bathe a newborn. The stove: two small gas burners and a roasting and broiling *drawer*. That was it. And from there Mother Murai fed nine people for ten hours. I suspected that behind the stove a cadre of helpers busied themselves whipping up dishes, and that they passed them through a secret drawer to mother Murai, but of course I was wrong. I've seen $100,000 Manhattan kitchens that don't feed as many people as much food in an entire year as Mother Murai fed her family that one night. In America it is common that at some point in a gathering the nucleus of the party moves to the kitchen, but in Japan the kitchen is entirely the realm of the chef. There is no talk or drinking to be done in the kitchen; the kitchen is for cooking.

At three in the afternoon I was very drunk from sake. It's normal for Westerners to drink sake with a beer on the side, using the whiskey-beer chaser model. But for the Japanese, beer is the warm-up drink and when you switch to sake you remain in the land of rice wine, unless you choose to switch to whiskey or vodka or *shochu*, but you never revert to beer. Katsunori, Sachiyo's brother-in-law, explained this to me and insisted on filling my glass every time the level dropped below half. For some reason it hadn't occurred to me that the only way not to drink was to keep a full glass in front of me. (That must be the answer to a Zen koan, or the first step in a Japanese twelve-step program.) But I did not mind my hours in the rice-wine bath—sake has always created for me a lucid and cheery drunkenness free of the melancholy, dread, and blindness that, for instance, whiskey might create. Sake also tastes better. Drinking sake is like taking a shower under a waterfall in Glacier National Park in the middle of July. Drinking whiskey is like swimming a Manhattan sewer line from Harlem to Chelsea in the middle of August.

After he filled my glass yet again I told Katsunori that I needed some exercise, and he and his daughters decided that we should play Wiffle ball. The problem was my legs were locked in place beneath me in the Japanese style. We were at a low table with an electric hearth beneath it turned on high, so my legs were aflame. I hadn't sat like this since roughly eighth grade, and I was certain that any sudden movement would cause my knees to explode. But Ren and Rui, Katsunori's daughters, were jumping on my back and dragging me to my feet before I could protest.

In the gravel yard next door we four played Wiffle ball. The two girls versus the two grown men. Advantage: girls. Renchan blasted my first pitch across the street and into the tall weeds. Out-of-the-park homer. Ruichan was a few years younger, and I thought that my split-fingered fastball would astonish her. But after the two girls had combined for nine home runs in a row—one inside the park by Ruichan, a true speed demon—the grown men gave the title to the young girls.

The brisk January weather and the minor physical activity of being battered at the mound by a twelve-year-old and her nine-year-old sister had brought me back to my senses. I felt hearty, like a competitor, and I was ready to eat again.

At the table two sukiyaki hot pots awaited our arrival. A riot of vegetables, meats, and noodles were piled high on plates, a Mt. Fuji of gastronomical excess. The beef was cut paper thin and was deeply marbled. The neatly stacked enoki mushrooms were perfect specimens that looked like an advancing battalion of soldiers—thin, muscular soldiers with white helmets atop their heads. The small bricks of *mochi* (rice cake) were a Murai family sukiyaki variation. They looked like pieces of stone from which Michelangelo would have been happy to carve miniatures. But we were going to cook and eat them. I've always been more of an eater than a sculptor.

Sukiyaki is a family meal. When S and I had dated we often fantasized about the trip we'd take to Japan together. But I was a broke college student and couldn't afford the fare from San Francisco to Tokyo, nor could I afford the time off. When I ended the relationship, on Easter 1998, I still had not been to Tokyo with her to visit her family.

So this was my first visit to Tokyo since late 1977, when my family moved back to California after my father's four-year stint at an Air Force base on the outskirts of the city (a base that was once a Japanese jet-plane factory). In Tokyo my family had often eaten sukiyaki together, both at home and at a restaurant just off base. The years in Japan were the last years that my family functioned well as a unit—the return to America was the beginning of the end of us. It would usher in my father's retirement from the Air Force and a series of career and business failures, his increasing distance from any sort of fathering role (other than disciplinarian), his blatant infidelities, and, finally, his violent split from my mother and my younger sister and me, the two children who were still at home. In 1977 my father was thirty-five, my same age today. He worked to pay two mortgages and support a family of six. There are some days when I understand the burdens that broke him and I forgive him, but most days I think: *What a fantastic blessing, a healthy family of six, four children and a wife who loved you—why did you fuck it all up?*

Today my parents are friends, and when I visit northern California I get together with my two sisters and our parents for family meals. We usually eat Thai food or Mexican. A Japanese meal together would be too much for us all. These meals are exclusively about reliving the past—the good stuff of the past, the zany and humorous memories are rehashed at family meals: the time Tami fell asleep on the toilet and the whole neighborhood spent three hours looking for her; the time Kim ate an entire jar of kimchi and earned the nickname Kimchi Kim; the time the front wheel on my motocross bicycle flew off, midwheelie, and bounced down the street in front of me—and a Japanese meal, I think, would revivify my father's failure at keeping his family intact, the very thing fathers are supposed to do.

Thus, the sukiyaki preparations in front of me were not simply sustenance, they were memory and loss. And so we ate. The Murai family made me feel as one of them. We filled the hot plates with slices of onion. In any culture the smell of sautéing onion is the smell of home and warmth, the base of so many dishes, the start of it all. And so it was. Once the onions were sautéed we added the sukiyaki sauce, made from soy, sake, sugar, and dashi. The sauce reached a low boil and we added enoki and shiitake mushrooms, red pepper, Napa cabbage, leek, seared tofu, *udon* noodles, jellyfish noodles, and thinly sliced beef. Once an item was cooked we removed it from the hot pot and dipped it in raw egg before eating it. We did this for an hour, drinking throughout. Renchan and Ruichan drank Kids' Beer (it's actually lemonade) and toasted along with the adults. We toasted the food, the chef, and one another.

Long after we had finished the sukiyaki, Mother Murai continued to send plates of food to the table: sashimi, sushi, a fresh plate of gyoza. If I never left the table, I'd never stop eating. The last train from Gotanno station to Shinjuku left at 11:47 PM. I made the train, barely. I was on my way to a Shinjuku hotel. But I knew that a new home was behind me at the Murai residence. I knew that while eating sukiyaki and gyoza with the Murai family I'd also been healing myself, making peace with my memories of the last great days of my childhood, making peace with my brother's death and the relationship with S that I'd unnecessarily doomed. At the Murai family table there was no room for despair—only for big appetites, and large, sweet hearts. We'd all been fed.

A few days ago I received a call from S, and she told me that she's pregnant and that she and her husband will have their child in California and then move to Japan. They intend to live in the mountains, off the grid, close to the earth. And next week I will attend my brother's daughter's high school graduation. So in a life we suffer the deaths of loved ones, and we might, as I did, ruin perfectly lovely relationships. But also there is rebirth, and movement, and the hope, for me at least, that meals like those I have shared with the Murai family will satisfy more than just my appetite.

RECIPE

Murai Family Sukiyaki

serves 4 to 6

Sukiyaki is a family-style meal prepared at the table. You'll want to use a deep cooking dish that will hold the broth and allow room for a heavy simmer. There are hot plates made specifically for sukiyaki and another Japanese dish, *shabu-shabu*, and you can also use a gas burner and a deep saucepan.

INGREDIENTS:

1–2 pounds high-quality beef, thinly sliced
1 package jellyfish noodles
1 package *udon* noodles
3 red peppers cut into 1-inch pieces
10 shiitake mushrooms; if large, cut in half
½ pound enoki mushrooms
2 large yellow onions, sliced
2 packages tofu, cut into 1-inch pieces
10–12 pieces of *mochi* (Japanese rice cake)

SUKIYAKI SAUCE:

3 tablespoons soy sauce
3 tablespoons sake
3 tablespoons sugar
1 cup dashi (Japanese stock, widely available)

Mix these ingredients in a bowl and set aside.

Place raw eggs (best if organic and fresh), one per guest, in small dipping bowl.

Heat one tablespoon of cooking oil over medium-high heat and sauté the onions, 4 to 5 minutes. Add the sukiyaki sauce to cooking vessel and bring to a heavy simmer. Now, each diner chooses items he or she would like to eat and adds them to the broth using chopsticks. When the food has reached desired state (medium rare, etc.), remove, dip in raw egg, eat, and enjoy. This is a great leisurely meal. Have more sukiyaki sauce on hand to replace what cooks away. Special tools: a mesh spoon to remove tofu and *mochi*.

It's simple to adjust the ingredients according to the size of your party and the size of the attending appetites. Serve with beer and sake. You might serve gyoza and/or sashimi as appetizers. These dishes can also be on the table throughout the meal.

Rummy

A. J. RATHBUN

*There's naught no doubt so much the spirit calms as rum
and true religion.* —LORD BYRON

In second grade, while attending the rural Santa Fe School
outside of McPherson, Kansas, I wrote a report on Thomas
Jefferson. Beyond delving into the mysteries of the dumb-
waiter, the two-faced clock, the automatic door, the revolv-
ing chair, and the apple picker (all of which seemed much
more interesting to me at eight than the fact that he wrote the
Declaration of Independence), I wandered into a list of the
contents of his wine cellar: fifteen bottles of Madeira, four of

"Lisbon wine for common use," fifty-four bottles of cider, and eighty-three of rum. Up until this point, I associated rum with pirates. What a shock then that Jefferson, one of the fathers of our country (as I would inform my class the next week), was a rummy.

My parents weren't teetotalers, but ours was a beer-and-wine household—the one exception being when my grandma dropped by for holiday occasions bearing a quart of Old Crow and a two-liter bottle of Coke. To discover that a historical figure such as Jefferson would have a cellar (a place I expected a Ping-Pong table should be) full of rum opened my young Kansan mind to the idea that liquor might hold a position of strange prestige in the adult world.

It wasn't odd for Jefferson to have such a cache of rum on hand. Beer and beer-styled potions had dominated the colonial drinking landscape in the sixteenth century, but by the late seventeenth century the American drinker started pouring distilled spirits. This shift was seismic, as nearly 90 percent of the population, young and old, believed not only in alcohol's ability to raise the spirit but also in its curative properties. Rum stumbled a little in the race of popular "strong waters" in America (the first rum distillery didn't open until around 1700 in Boston), but its relative obscurity didn't last, for three reasons. First, it was cheap. Second, it mixed well, instigating hot buttered rums, rum punches, spiced rums, and egg- and other nogs. Third, it didn't taste like poison.

It's true, rum rode hell and high water as a sailor's favorite tonic before coming ashore. But rum's complex personality was already present even in its harshest ancestors. When temperatures are sinking, rum echoes a sun that glares hot over sugarcane fields, creating islands, palm trees, and sultry sand in the imagination of even the most landlocked drinker huddled up against an oak bar. Rum's a lush dark wisp of vanilla on the tongue's tip, followed by a quick fire in the back of the throat, a welcoming burn that says: Yes, you belong with us, on the stern of the ship, on the edge of the feral world, where laughter and passion are common currency. Rum lives in the bright bonfire's midst, where other liquors are ash. It's an adventure scented by syrup, cinnamon, and the hint of danger.

Mainly derived from molasses, a by-product of the sugar-refining process and in the seventeenth century an inexpensive import from the West Indies, rum also made economic sense. For early American rum distillers (though there are none today, at one point in the 1700s there were thirty rum distillers around Boston and Rhode Island), it led to large profits. Before long, American-made rum wasn't just a colonial hit, as around six hundred thousand gallons were being exported annually.

As the rum trade surged in the 1700s, it developed a kinship with the most appalling form of colonial big business—slavery. Most historians now doubt the existence of the infamous "triangle trade," which supposedly involved the same ships carrying molasses from the Caribbean to New England, then acquiring rum from New England distilleries to take to Africa, and finally picking up slaves to take back to the British West Indies. Each ship may not have followed that route as neatly as the "triangle" suggests, but nevertheless big money was being made by companies trafficking in rum, slaves, and molasses. Cheaply priced New England rum proliferated in Upper Guinea and the Gold Coast, enriching colonial coffers but also helping to enslave millions. In addition, American rum, less expensive and smoother tasting, rode more traditional West Indian rum, gin, brandy, and other liquors out of Gold Coast larders. The trading of rum, molasses, and slaves was a profitable business for years, and most people simply ignored the human sacrifices, echoing the British poet William Cowper when he wrote, "I pity them greatly, but I must be mum / For how could we do without sugar and rum?"

Don't be fooled by rum's mixability, or its sultry presence in fruity, blended drinks and Rupert Holmes's piña colada song. Rum has hung out with tough crowds. It's even had murder hung on its name, as in an 1829 poem recounting the dying words of a murderer named Moses Lion: "In confessing his guilt & his crime / He imputes it to whiskey and rum." Although no one can pinpoint the moment of its birth and christening, the name itself originates either from the Latin word for sugarcane, *Saccarum*, or the old gypsy *rum*, meaning "grand" or "potent." It's worn other monikers, too, most a reflection of its dangerous nature: *Kill-Divil, hydra-monster, rumbowling, cursed liquor, rhum*, and, of course, *that demon rum.*

Demon or not, in the 1700s rum started its own revolution, shifting drinking preferences of American settlers new and old. Soon the top beverage in taverns and hearthsides, rum reformed tastes in a particularly American way. Not only was it affordable for the distiller to make, but cheaper than beer for the tavern owner to store (taking up less space), and therefore less expensive for taverngoers. However, more than economics fueled rum's popularity. Rum mirrored the democratic soul of the colonies—its potent discharge could be savored straight, mixed with two spoonfuls of warm water and cloves, or poured into a punch. While beer and wine held distinct class connections, all Americans when drinking rum might imagine they were sharing a drink, however distantly, with Thomas Jefferson. Accordingly, both the lower and upper classes could be found, like the captain in Dickens's *Dombey and Son*, "taking a glass of warm rum-and-water at a tavern close by, to collect [their] thoughts."

When the Revolutionary War broke out, the British blockaded many Atlantic ports, making it hard, if not impossible, to import molasses and export rum. At the same time, feeling that Pacific pull, settlers started moving out to the western frontier. Due to the lack of cushy packing materials, rum didn't travel well on the bumpy trail (both casks and bottles were always at risk of breaking). Moreover, the abundance of grain on the frontier gave whiskey an opening into the populace's glasses, hearts, and pocketbooks. By the early 1800s, rum's moment at the top of the booze mountain was past.

Rum never wholly plummeted out of the cocktail equation; nor did it regain prominence. Like its sister spirits, rum took its temperance-movement lumps in the nineteenth and early twentieth centuries, back-doored into smoky speakeasies during Prohibition, and then got shaken, stirred, and poured plentifully in the post-Prohibition years. While not as popular as gin, rum made the guest list of most mid-twentieth-century bars. In his 1941 *Drinking Guide and Ladies Companion*, cocktailian-about-town Crosby Gaige says, "It would be my opinion that in long range and diversified cocktail-mixing, the various rums make more sense, and present more opportunity for sound experiment, than any other basic liquor, except possibly gin. The latter is potent in spirit and fairly neutral in flavor, while rum has potency and is highly endowed with flavor and aromas." Gaige never mixed cocktails with vodka, or rum might have placed third (vodka's notable popularity coattails the 1940s and '50s Smirnoff company's "Moscow Mule" and "It Leaves You Breathless" ad campaigns). Gaige doesn't—some would say to his credit—list the piña colada among his rum cocktails, although he does include Fig Leaves for Two, the Cuban Caress, and the President Watson. (The last, made of Cuban rum, orange curaçao, dry vermouth, and grenadine, is followed by this advice: "Take a deep breath and prepare to meet the board of directors.")

After my second-grade Jefferson report, I suggested to my parents that, like children in the eighteenth century, I should have a daily rum ration: a snug cupful with milk at breakfast, five ounces on ice at dinner, and a sleepy mug of eggnog before bed. They didn't applaud the idea. My association with the tropical spirit waned until I began bartending at the Hibachi Hut in Manhattan, Kansas. (The Hut was named such because at its unsafe beginnings, flaming hibachi grills were brought to individual tables for its drunken guests to cook on.) Manhattan is a college town, and midwestern college-age men and women, I soon discovered, liked their drinks sugary and blended.

Rum's twentieth-century renaissance sailed in on Caribbean winds, naturally, facilitated by Hemingway's romanticized love of Cuban daiquiris and mojitos. In a letter to Ivan Kashkin, Papa H. expounded his rum views: "Before an attack who can say anything that gives you the momentary well-being that rum does? The only time it isn't good for you is when you write or when you fight. You have to do that cold. But it always helps my shooting. Modern life, too, is often a mechanical oppression and liquor is the only mechanical relief." Buoyed also by drinkers' expeditions to the island-influenced Florida coast, rum bounded back to the bar in pitchers of piña coladas, boosting bikini dreams and the aforementioned Top 40 hit. But as a bartender, the piña topped my most-hated-drink list. The people ordering them were almost always bad tippers, and so much syrup was involved that a sticky mess was the inevitable aftereffect.

Ironically, considering rum's history, the piña colada's inventor wasn't an islander, but a European. Ricardo Garcia or, some sources say, Ramon Marrero—the exact names of drink inventors are as elusive as a perfect mai tai—was born in Barcelona in 1914, and ran restaurants and bars in Spain before moving to San Juan, Puerto Rico, in 1954 to govern the bar at the Caribe Hilton Hotel. At the Caribe, guests received a complimentary cocktail of coconut juice, rum, and Coco Lopez (cream of coconut) served in a freshly cut coconut (a practice that needs a revival). Then the coconut-cutters union went on strike. Luckily, our intrepid bartender crafted a solution, serving the drinks in a fresh pineapple. Guests loved it, and a classic cocktail was born.

Eventually I succumbed to piña coladas. The merger of rum's Havana with sweet coconut and pineapple's tangy beach is too hard to resist—it still mesmerizes the way rum mesmerized the colonists. Today, one can choose between silver rum's silky clarity and light and the heavier-textured chocolate, oak, and spice of gold, dark, and brown rum. One could also take up with rum's feisty Brazilian cousin *cachaca* (fermented from sugarcane juice, as opposed to molasses) or rums flavored with coconut, mango, or citrus—all transport the drinker, if only for a while, to a brighter beach. There, as Derek Walcott says in his poem "The Liberator," "a sunbeam dances through brown rum bottles like a firefly through a thicket of cocoa." Though Jefferson's rum collection might still seem somewhat excessive, he'd be comfortable bellying up to a neighborhood bar in the twenty-first century, toasting with the other rummies.

RECIPE

The Piña Colada

Piña coladas are a group drink. If you want to drink rum solo, pick up a high-end brown rum and sip it over ice. But when the sun beats hard, call up a posse and get the blender whirring. This recipe isn't overly sweet, but it does have some of that sticky cream of coconut, so be careful of the countertops. If you don't have dark rum, you can make it with light rum only, but it won't be quite the same. You'll feel like you're in Miami, and not on an actual island. If the heavy cream makes your heart go pitter-patter a little too heavily, substitute soy milk.

INGREDIENTS:

1 ounce light rum
1 ounce dark rum
1 ounce heavy cream
½ cup pineapple juice
2 ounces Coco Lopez
1 cup crushed ice

Pour all ingredients into a blender; blend for 15 seconds or until the mixture is smooth.

Pour into a 12-ounce glass (if you have a special poco-grande glass—a 12- to 13-ounce stemmed glass with a wave-and-a-half bowl—use it). Garnish with a pineapple wedge, and, if you really want to, a cherry.

Feel free to double, triple, or even quadruple this recipe if you have a rocking blender. That way you'll spend more time drinking—and less time making—the piñas.

Beating the Heat

RICH KING

As the longer, hotter days of summer melt into fall, I contemplate the past few months, my first full summer on the isle of Manhattan. One can perhaps think of more desirable islands on which to spend the four months of the Northern Hemisphere's closest approach to the sun, the sort with palm-shaded beaches or cool, rugged coastlines. One might choose a certain purity for her surrounding bodies of water rather than the stew that is both the East and Hudson rivers. But we did not. My boyfriend and I stayed. We sweltered. We panted. We boiled and broiled and very nearly blistered. We were consistently agitated, if not aggravated. We fled to our rooftop, a questionable decision given the closer proximity to the sun.

It was there, while we dripped and soaked, considering how soon would be too soon for the next shower, that we took upon ourselves a quest. Our endeavor would be to find the very best drink, the ultimate refresher. It would be the quaff to rescue us from our financially imposed marooning. We spent a day in preparation: charting our course of coolants while knocking back several of our still-favorite refreshers, the lowest-end lager.

Having owned and tended bars in Oregon, we both fancy ourselves well versed in the cocktail. Actually, the Oregon climate creates many a good drinker, the practice stemming from attempted escape from the eight-month hyper-precipitative winter. We culled our experience and considered many directions and destinations. The Cape Codder seemed a bit staid, if not pedestrian. The gimlet, my family's summer-sailing thermos-filler, was too much work without all the kids to squeeze fresh limes, and you can guess how we feel about those nasty bottled varieties of lime juice. We pointed ourselves in a more southerly direction, below the Mason-Dixon Line, to climes ever closer to the sun and thus to cultures, of necessity, ever better in the art of refreshment.

We went nearer the equator, this time swilling margaritas. Unfortunately, this potable set us to quarreling and brought us a few too many headache-filled mornings-after. Our recollections and geographic explorations landed us, quite literally, in our old backyard, in the midst of a cocktail memory carried with us from a more verdant and much cooler Pacific North-west.

This Best Drink is a Left Coast spin on an old standard. It is an intersection of global cooling remedies and a sort of union of two summer favorites. It winks wryly at its southern sire, the mint julep. It nods and smiles fondly at its more demure and hospitable dame, the gin fizz.

My boyfriend insists the fizz was probably developed for the ladies, as it is lighter, somehow softer and more sippable than most "manly" cocktails. Bill Boothby, author of the 1930 classic *"Cocktail Bill" Boothby's World Drinks and How to Mix Them*, wrote, "Plain fizzes are recommended as eye-openers for the morning after the night before." Had we only known this at the time of the margarita experiment . . .

Fizz drinks are generally made with gin and always with soda. They can come plain, silver (with egg white), golden (with yolk), or royal (using both). I imagine my grandparents in another era, he a medical student at Tufts, down to visit stunning Christine, a Neshanic flower, a young model in the city. Both are all adither riding trains toward the old Pennsyl-vania Station and dashing off to meet friends for brunch over a Diamond Fizz (gin, lemon, sugar, and champagne) or a Bar-celona (gin, lime, sherry, and soda, with just a spot of sugar syrup), the effervescence fueling an already bubbling week-end of romance. Somehow, sadly, the fizz has dropped off the cocktail map. Though I am certain that somewhere, perhaps in an overgrown garden, there is a contingent of nubile young things softly sipping fizzes. And if not, there ought to be.

While the fizz tickled us, it lacked a certain oomph that we were looking for. So we moved on to the mint julep.

Concoctions called *julebs* (Arabic) or *gulabs* (Persian) emerged from Middle Eastern medicine and cuisine in the first half of the last millennium. The words literally mean "scented water." These potions were generally sweetened water flavored with aromatics such as rose or orange. Some were used as curative tinctures and others, in more decadent circumstances, for refreshment. The New World adapters of this "medicine" added spirituous liquors and mint to the mixture, thus creating the mint julep. The cocktail can be found in the notes of British travelers as far back as 1803. Joseph Lanza, in his text *The Cocktail: The Influence of Spirits on the American Psyche*, cites Mr. John Davis, a visitor and tutor in Virginia, defining the julep as "a dram of spirituous liquor that has mint in it taken by Virginians of a morning."

Let us take a moment to extol the virtues of the herb by itself, without the company of alcohol and sugar. In antiquity, the Romans crowned themselves with wreaths of the spear-shaped mint leaves. Ovid considered it the very symbol of hospitality. Greek and Arab philosophers and medical men championed mint for its restorative and invigorating powers. In the Far East, mint is found in the cuisines of both India and Vietnam as a counternote to the hotter flavors of peppers and ginger. Arab cultures also cook with mint to balance the heat found in other foods and serve it brewed as a refreshing after-meal tea.

In American cocktail history, the morning seems to have been the appropriate time of day to start one's "cooling." In *Eating, Drinking and Visiting in the South: An Informal History*, Joe Gray Taylor relates the visit of Mr. William Russell to the Burnside plantation in Louisiana. On this visit, Russell learned that the julep was the "panacea for all the evils of climate." At Burnside, the cure began before the morning meal. Upon bringing him a third cup, a servant informed Russell that he "had better take this, because it'll be the last he make[s] before breakfast." The belief in the curative power of the julep cannot be far off base. Alcohol works to quickly reduce body temperature. So the whiskey, combined with the invigorating properties of mint and the obvious coolness of ice, makes one hell of a tincture—that means cure—against the heat.

As with most things Southern, the mint julep demands a certain protocol. Propriety dictates that juleps not be served before the end of May, which corresponds conveniently with the running of the Kentucky Derby and the Kentucky Oaks, where the prize is not one silver cup but one dozen sterling julep tumblers. The New College at Oxford observes this seasonality as well. Mint Julep Day in the motherland is in the beginning of June, though this event surely pales when compared with the imbibing associated with the Derby. No less than eighty thousand mint juleps (two thousand gallons of cocktail, one hundred and fifty bushels of mint, and sixty tons of shaved ice) are consumed during that weekend event.

The following is the recipe for a full batch (hosts that we are) of eight mint juleps.

It comes from Woodruff Reserve, the bourbon distiller that is an official sponsor of the Kentucky Derby.

Mint Juleps, a whole batch

serves 8

INGREDIENTS:

2 cups sugar
2 cups boiling hot water
8 sprigs fresh mint, plus extra for garnish
crushed ice
Kentucky bourbon
8 chilled silver julep cups

Make a simple syrup by adding the sugar to the boiling water, stirring until dissolved. Gently bruise and place 8 sprigs of mint in the mixture. Refrigerate overnight to infuse. Make one julep at a time by filling a julep cup with ice, adding 1 tablespoon mint syrup and 2 ounces bourbon. Stir rapidly with a spoon so as to frost the outside of the cup. Garnish with a sprig of fresh mint. Serve with short, fat straws.

Protocol inherently breeds conflict. Indeed, there is conflict among mixologists over the proper making of the julep. Some recipes call for the mint to be muddled in the glass for each individual cocktail. This crushing of the mint, rather than a gentle bruising, brings out more of the volatile oils and thus a sharper or crisper cocktail. In this matter, Boothby advises that you consult your guest for her preference to avoid a potential insult. Legend has it that a Yank shaved nutmeg into someone's julep, thus setting off a course of events that eventually rent our nation in two. Other issues to consider are the shape and material of the containers, as some hold a longer frost and others afford a better noseful of those volatile oils. One might even consider, if only for a moment, an alternate liquor. Mint seems to work well with most other liquors, except maybe tequila, but we know where that liquor leaves us. In fact, Boothby suggests using gin, rum, whiskey, and brandy among the dozen or so juleps he lists. (*Note*: The first mint juleps were made with brandy, and it was not until the mid-1800s that this was supplanted by bourbon whiskey.) Truly, all that really matters is what an individual prefers, protocol and propriety be damned. But remember the essentials: sugar, alcohol, mint, ice, and straws.

Benjamin Franklin once quipped, "There can't be good living where there is not good drinking." After so much fizzing, then muddling, bruising, and infusing, we had indeed found good living. But not great living. There was still something missing, and that something was the spice of ginger. In the midst of the worst heat of the summer we had a joint flashback to a Portland cocktail simply called The Best Drink, which combines the effervescence of the fizz with the crispness of the julep and adds the exotic sting of ginger. Who knows what madman first mixed boiled ginger into this cocktail, but whoever it is, I'd like to kiss him.

What follows is the recipe for The Best Drink, a perfect tonic against all the evils of clime, whether one is below the Mason-Dixon Line or simply sweltering in the city. Our recipe comes from Saucebox in Portland, the originator of The Best Drink.

RECIPE

The Best Drink

INGREDIENTS:

6 fresh sprigs of mint, extra for garnish

1 ½ ounces lemon-lime (juices of lemon and lime in equal parts)

2 ounces gin

1 ounce simple syrup (see julep recipe)

1 ounce ginger brew (boil 1 quarter-pound fresh, peeled ginger in 1 cup water for 30 minutes; ginger ale can be substituted if no fresh ginger is available)

6 ½ ounces crushed ice

1 12-ounce chimney glass

In a pint glass, muddle 6 mint leaves with 1 ounce of crushed ice. To this add 1 ½ ounces lemon-lime, 2 ounces gin, and simple syrup to taste (usually 1 ounce will do). Cover and shake vigorously. Strain into a well-chilled chimney glass, add remaining crushed ice, and top with a float of ginger brew. Garnish with a sprig of mint and serve with a straw.

Drinking My Inheritance

SARA ROAHEN

My earliest memory of winter evenings in Wisconsin is of being in a canoe-size toboggan shuttling down the slalom course of Aunt Nancy and Uncle Larry's front yard toward a congregation of evergreens. The grown-ups would pile on the toboggan with me, their warm-sour brandy breath visible in the pinching cold as they talked incessantly about all the fun we were having. Hours later, my younger sister, Stephanie, and I curled up on a makeshift bed in the living room, listening to the faraway yelps and squeals of the grown-ups as they sprinted, nude, from Uncle Larry's incendiary sauna to a snowbank outside and back again, pausing only to refresh a cocktail. Stephanie dozed off effortlessly, but I lay awake, petrified that a cold-induced heart attack would orphan me at any moment.

Their choice of cocktail was seasonless, but activities at the weekend-long parties changed with the weather. Come summer, the snow melted to reveal a swimming pool surrounded on all sides by overgrown Christmas trees and rented plots of feed corn. The men shot at clay pigeons all day as their women

Sara Roahen

pretended to watch, but Stephanie and I stayed poolside. While she perfected her back dive, I dripped dry beneath the porch with plates of sour cream cucumbers and a prickling sunburn. It was impossible to gauge back then—or now—which was most to blame for my bouts of summer insomnia: the green shag carpeting that poked through Aunt Nancy's satin sheets against my blistered skin; the orchestra of moths searing in the bug light outside; Jefferson County cops triaging drunk drivers over Uncle Larry's radio scanner; or the grown-ups' howling as they drained the swimming pool in a cannonball contest. Heart attacks didn't worry me in the summertime. Instead, I was sure one of them would crack open a skull on the pool's cement lip.

Occasionally these weekends terminated at Sunday Mass, where we thanked the Lord in person for so much fun. But mostly Stephanie and I feigned sleep when Aunt Nancy woke up on Sunday mornings, praying that instead of rousing us for church she would switch on the Christian radio station she claimed would save our souls. It was a weak substitute for church, she admitted as she shuffled back to bed, but at least it would keep us out of hell for another seven days. If you had asked me at the time to what we owed this stroke of heathen fortune, I would have answered: Uncle Larry's brandy old-fashioned sweets.

These were not the gentlemanly whiskey old-fashioneds of water splashes and sugar cubes and *absolutely nothing carbonated* that cocktail academics believe was invented in the mid-

1800s in Kentucky. These old-fashioneds were big and stiff, as generous as the beers sold at Lambeau Field, with a pitch-perfect balance of sweet and bitter, alcoholic warmth, and ice cube chill. And they were apparently refreshing enough to drink all night long. Uncle Larry still measures his old-fashioneds in brandy glugs and shakes of bitters and finishes them with 7Up. He stirs them with cinnamon sticks and garnishes them with maraschino cherries. While he is considered the authority on old-fashioneds in our family—his heavily researched recipe is still the platonic ideal for us all—his typically Wisconsin version of the drink is to the original highbrow cocktail what a double espresso latte with whipped cream and cinnamon is to a cup of joe. It's bigger, it's sweeter, it's got more spice. Its smooth base, brandy, is at least as different from whiskey as an espresso shot is from a straight-up French roast. Except around the pool, where only plastic UW-Wisconsin Badger football cups were allowed, these old-fashioneds always came in ice-packed glasses painted with pheasants soaring over marshes and spaniels pointing at flocks of plump, deaf quail.

The garnishes were the greatest thrill for little girls. Phosphorescent, brandy-marinated cherries shimmered under the melting ice in sweating glasses like brightly painted fishing lures. But, like Mom's holiday bourbon balls—which always ended up spit into a poinsettia napkin—the cherries were deceptively harsh. So we gnawed on the cinnamon sticks, which were never alcoholic, just spicy and wet. To this day, when throwing a cinnamon stick into a pot of black beans, I find myself back in the campfire air of Aunt Nancy and Uncle Larry's wood-heated home.

While I grew up around brandy old-fashioneds, my father's parents hadn't even heard of brandy before eloping from Ohio to Wisconsin in 1939. It became their drink of choice when they found that their new friends kept no other liquor in the house. Brandy consumption in Wisconsin has always been higher per capita than in any other state, but a growing taste for spiced rum, flavored vodka, and specialty martinis among the younger Wisconsin social-drinking circles has led to a sharp decline in statewide brandy sales. This drop is causing panic among brandy producers. Since Wisconsin's bordering states have such similar geographical, socioeconomic, and ethnic breakdowns, they have never figured out what originally drove Wisconsinites to covet it. Therefore, they don't know how to ensure that our passion doesn't fizzle out. Says Gary Heck, owner of Korbel Brandy, "It must have been what the wagon had on it when it first got there."

It appears that the wagon was brimming. Generations of Wisconsinites have ensured that brandy's uses are boundless. Especially in rural areas, bartenders often use brandy in place of other brown liquors without warning. Natives expect it, but out-of-state customers learn to specify brands when ordering a bourbon and water or a whiskey sour. Most brandy old-fashioned drinkers I know drink them sweet, made with 7Up, but you can also order them made with sour mix (a brandy old-fashioned sour), with water, with seltzer, or with half 7Up, half seltzer. This half-and-half version is called a brandy old-fashioned Press, short for Presbyterian—though no one seems to know the connection between Presbyterians and brandy old-fashioneds.

By the time I landed my first job, brandy old-fashioneds were as embedded in my consciousness as frostbite and fried cheese curds. Most bars wouldn't let kids my age onto the premises to use the pay phone, much less to work, but since the management at private golf clubs in Wisconsin didn't believe in age discrimination, I brought in more cash cocktail waitressing the summer I turned eighteen than I've made during any three-month period since. I also became unusually attached to the smell of sticky brandy and bitters drying on a cork-lined cocktail tray. I still didn't drink old-fashioneds, preferring Mogan David at the time, but it became clear that a fanatical allegiance to the cocktail was not particular to my family. Thursday's men's nights at the golf club were the rowdiest and most lucrative for me, but it was during Friday night fish fries that my fellow statesmen and -women most openly indulged their affections for our regional cherry-brown drink. Friday night fish fries in Wisconsin are as ubiquitous as brats at a Brewers game, and everyone knows the protocol. You always take as much of the family as you can, you always take the good car, and you always show up early for a drink in the bar. Club members whose aperitif preference wasn't a brandy old-fashioned were such a minority that more than a decade later I still remember these anomalies: the retired couple with a powder-blue golf cart who only drank vodka tonics; the Miller Genuine Draft–swilling lout who was an ass pincher on Thursdays and a family man on Fridays; and the leather-skinned golf pro who separated himself from the hacks by drinking whiskey old-fashioneds with olives.

Today there's a very new-millennium martini menu at Club 26, a supper club just south of Fort Atkinson where my parents found the fried cod so superior that they held their wedding reception there on a Friday evening in 1970. Yet the club's bartenders still make so many brandy old-fashioneds that they prepare for Friday evenings by mixing gallons of simple syrup and bitters (not to be confused with the appalling old-fashioned blends sold in Wisconsin liquor stores next to the piña colada, Bloody Mary, and margarita mixes). I doubt a Club 26 bartender has ever made an old-fashioned in that sodaless manner that characterized them in nineteenth-century Kentucky, and that still characterizes them in forty-nine states. If a customer requested one, the staff would probably react with the same confusion that strikes bartenders outside the borders of Wisconsin when you ask for an old-fashioned made with brandy and 7Up even as they're reaching for the whiskey and the sugar cubes. At Club 26, you get an above-average if weak version of Uncle Larry's old-fashioned, minus the wildfowl glasses and the cinnamon stick (both homemade touches). The first one goes down like a Shirley Temple while we pretend to consider Club 26's newer menu items—chicken schnitzel, salmon with sauerkraut—and then agree on the cod.

I've heard it said that a Wisconsin fish fry isn't genuine if it doesn't come with a relish tray of raw vegetables, sour cherry peppers, olives, and little pickles. Club 26 ditched the relish tray for deep-fried dinner rolls long ago, but the centerpiece is still nuggets of firm, bleach-white cod fished from oceans far from the Great Lakes and wrapped in clingy sheaths of brown batter that are more chewy than crisp, but never greasy. A brandy old-fashioned remains the natural accompaniment to fried fish for many of us, but now that Kendall Jackson and his California friends have infiltrated nearly every wood-paneled supper club across the state, even my grandparents occasionally fall for research suggesting that wine will conquer the wicked effects of fried foods.

Nevertheless, there's little other sign of a brandy recession in any generation of my family. The moment we enter the house on a visit, before Mom can set the table with cheddar cheese soup and macaroni salad, Dad asks, "Regular 7Up or diet?" (Some Wisconsinites do count calories.) My cousin's husband, Doug, Uncle Larry's nephew by marriage, is another artisan of the regional cocktail. His patent-worthy technique, the results of which we taste every Christmas Eve before presents, involves holding the glass up to the stained woodwork in the bar he built himself. If the woodwork is darker than the drink, he adds more brandy.

Those panicking brandy makers might also take heart if they saw the solid wall of brandy displayed at a certain truck stop just outside Wisconsin Dells. It's the last place I know of to buy a bottle on the way up to the home where Aunt Nancy and Uncle Larry retired among the osprey and eagles of Lake Castle Rock. Their weekend-long parties have gone the way of Badger football victories, but I have noticed a sauna built suspiciously close to a sliding glass door in the basement. Still the barrel-chested, baritone-voiced man of my youth, Uncle Larry mixes everyone two old-fashioneds before we head out to their favorite local fish fry. I'm the only one who can't finish both. When I was younger, my dad used to stabilize his Friday night old-fashioned-for-the-road between his thighs as he drove; I would fret in the backseat, longing for the day when I could take the wheel. He still protests when I offer to drive—the restaurant is just a few miles down the road, after all, and cars have cup holders now. During dinner I pour my fourth old-fashioned into Aunt Nancy's empty glass, completely undetected. It has always been a combination of thrill and dread trying to keep pace with the grown-ups.

Most of the family in the generation older than mine is still fairly young, settling down but not nearly ready to give up. They aren't sure yet what part of our family they would pass on if I asked them to. There are no cows to milk, no taffy to make, no shoes to repair in our clan. No law firm. No corner store. But I'm older now than they were when we used to pile on that toboggan, and I have reached an age when finding something to claim as ours before it becomes just me feels crucial. It's a primal impulse, a nostalgic ache for things that aren't gone quite yet—something like the urge to procreate, only in reverse. So I thought about my inheritance options and came to a conclusion that surprises even me: I'm taking the old-fashioned. Taking the garnishes and everything else that comes with it. It was there from the beginning anyhow. I just needed the recipe.

RECIPE

Uncle Larry's Brandy Old-Fashioned Sweet

Most brandy old-fashioned makers I know are partial to a particular brand (Uncle Larry likes Christian Brothers), but any inexpensive brandy will do. It's essential to make ice in the largest cubes possible; the balance of bitters, brandy, and sweetness is easily diluted, and the kind of nubby ice sold by the bag melts too quickly. Lastly, most store-bought bar syrups are either saccharine-sweet or have a plasticky flavor. After years of empirical research Uncle Larry found one to fit his taste, Sweet 10, but you can also make your own simple syrup by heating equal parts water and sugar on the stovetop and stirring just until the sugar dissolves. For easy access, store the syrup in a squirt bottle or other covered vessel with a pour spout.

INGREDIENTS:

Liberal 2 jiggers (3 ounces) brandy
4 or 5 strong dashes Angostura bitters
1 teaspoon simple syrup
½ of one 2-inch cinnamon stick (split it lengthwise)
6 ounces (half a can) cold 7Up
Maraschino cherries to taste

Fill a 12-ounce tumbler to the top with ice cubes and pour in brandy. Add bitters and simple syrup; stir with cinnamon stick, leaving the stick in the glass. Top off the drink with 7Up and stir again with a long-handled bar spoon. Garnish with maraschino cherries, either floating or skewered on a toothpick.

A Season in Elk Country

LYNNE SAMPSON

I have read that, in Africa, when the body of an antelope, which all its life ate only leaves and grass and drank nothing but wild water, is first opened, the fragrance is almost too sweet, too delicate, too beautiful to be borne. It is a moment which hunters must pass through carefully, with concentrated and even religious attention, if they are to reach the other side, and go onwith their individual lives. —MARY OLIVER, *White Pine*

On a late October Monday morning in Joseph, Oregon, there was no traffic on the highway that passes through the eight blocks of town on its dead-end route to Wallowa Lake. The Joseph Fly Shoppe and the Corner Bookstore were closed; Timberline Realty open but empty. Outside the false-fronted Cheyenne Café, a few pickup trucks with hay bales and pacing border collies awaited the last farmers and ranchers huddled over coffee cups inside. Beside the café, a narrow walkway cracked from frost led to Salon Joseph, a shuttered, barn-board space where I had a 9 AM appointment for a manicure.

We were alone, Quinn Casaray and I. Country music played from a boom box set on a wood cookstove, and the air smelled of eucalyptus and hair spray. Quinn pulled my right hand from the warm, sudsy water and said, "I got a cow tag." I looked up from my hands.

"Deer?" I asked.

"No, elk. It's my first time," she said. I studied her as she cut my cuticles, a hip, twenty-two-year-old natural beauty with shining auburn hair, ivory freckled skin, and a thin, muscular frame. In high school, Quinn was a princess of the Chief Joseph Days Rodeo Court, but this fall she was more interested in hunting than horsemanship. She told me how hard it was to get a permit to hunt cow elk and how her grandfather had scolded her once when he saw her blink as she raised her gun. "Never close your eyes," he said. "You'll do nothing but injure an animal that way." I pictured her out in the chilled, sunburnt canyon, posed with her rifle over the corpse of an enormous and still-warm elk, smiling.

A newcomer and city transplant, I wasn't attuned to the subtle shifts leading into elk season. The Best Western hotel announcing "Welcome Hunters." Jerry's Market adding butchering and meat-hanging services to its stock of iceberg lettuce, Doritos, and 7Up. The encircling of camouflage hats and rifle shells around the cash register at Joseph Hardware. The slow parade of pickups down Main Street, the shadow of a gun rack behind the driver's head. Each sign was like golden glints of the sugar maples in the New England woods before the landscape bursts into full color.

In the Wallowa Valley, where the snow-capped wilderness is our closest neighbor, the elk inform casual conversation from the post office to the Safeway checkout line. At Cloud 9 Bakery, Bill, a wildlife photographer and artist, laughed about his unsuccessful bow hunt. At her bed-and-breakfast, Sandy described how she killed a seven-point bull elk and how it brought her husband to tears. As other small-town newspapers cover high school football, the *Wallowa County Chieftain* publishes a hunting report and photos of the latest big bull-elk kill. By the time the first snows fall on the wheat fields, elk is on everyone's mind, whether you own a gun or not.

Elk season captivates not by what is seen but by what is unseen. Elk live around us, but not among us, as their deer cousins do. In summer, they dwell in the inaccessible high alpine meadows; in winter they retreat into the folds of canyons. The elk have kept their wildness. They do not crowd the shoulders of roadways and pose a driving hazard. They do not poach my garden, or camp underneath my apple tree, waiting for windfall. They do not beg from, and delight, the summer tourists at the lake. Sighting a herd is a gift.

The week before the opening of the first elk rifle season, driving back to town from a hike, I stopped for a Chevrolet pickup truck parked in the narrow, winding road. Two men, wearing plaid shirts and suspenders, were looking up at the hillside, one of them through binoculars. I pulled up alongside.

"What are you looking at?"

"An elk herd," said the one without the binoculars, who kept looking up toward the ridge. I could barely make out five slow-moving brown specks, melding with the tans and grays of the sun-blanched grasses and lichen-covered rocks. "I bet you're looking forward to next week," I said to them, ranchers I guessed, given their dusty truck and their attire. They both turned to look at me. "I haven't hunted in years," one said.

I saw my first elk fifty miles from there, as we chased cows out of my brother-in-law's wheat field one July. The last Charolais evicted and the fence mended, we were three abreast in the pickup, surfing the fallow field, when a dozen elk blazed across our path. The slant late-afternoon light illuminated the entire scene of wheat and cow and ponderosa pine with a glow like lantern light. It gleamed from the elks' bronze flanks for one moment before they were gone. In an instant they were there, and as suddenly not there, which, in their size and number, was magic. Only my brother-in-law, a lifelong farmer and hunter, spoke. "Sure are pretty this time of year," he said.

Teddy Roosevelt, the venerable hunter with a subspecies of Washington State elk named after him, admired elk as passionately as he hunted them. He wrote with the sensibility of a naturalist when he praised "the proud, graceful, half-timid, half-defiant bearing of an elk." It is this quiet nobility, this elusive nature of the majestic bulls and watchful cows that draws us to them. And none of their glory is diminished by a hunter's ability to kill one cleanly on a lucky day. The only shame is in a long shot or a slow kill, or worse, losing the track of a wounded animal. The elk is not a foe or a felon, like the cougar, bear, and coyote. It is an object of desire. Its beauty, power, and independence are what we crave for ourselves.

When I left Seattle to live in a town of one thousand people in the far eastern reaches of Oregon, friends worried about my cultural and culinary survival. "What will you do?" and "What will you eat?" were wrapped together in the same bundle of urban ignorance about modern life in the rural West. I harbored my own concerns that I was trading in farmers' market produce, fresh fish, and imported cheese for bison burgers, Jell-O molds, and Schwan's frozen food delivery. But I arrived in April, just when the morel season began. I searched for the secret places mushroom hunters guard like gold claims. The melting spring snows filled the rivers and generous fishermen shared rainbow trout. I realized that in the twenty-first-century West, you can't live off the grid, but you can eat off of it.

Slowly, I learned where to forage for my food: fresh eggs from the bookstore, boletus mushrooms from a potato farmer, heirloom apples from the orchard of an abandoned homestead. In early September, while camping near a just-ripened huckleberry patch, I ate as many tiny berries as I picked, one at a time. No two tasted alike. After the first pop of skin, there were a thousand degrees of sweetness and a journey of flavors, from musty to meaty. There was earth and sun and dung held captive in each berry, like a secret. It is this quality that makes us search out wild foods with a neediness that is beyond hunger. A Nez Perce man I know, raised on wild meat, can't bear the taste of beef.

By Thanksgiving, I was on an elk trail of my own. Back at the salon, Quinn told me how she shot her elk. "When they're hit in the heart, they run," she said. "I didn't know I killed it until it fell." At the health food store, the owner showed me her new freezer and opened it just wide enough for me to see neat packs of maroon meat inside. "That's our elk," she said, smiling. "My husband got it bow hunting," and then she let the door drop shut fast. Not for sale. An industrious Oregon pioneer once sold meat for ten cents a pound to Indians living on the reservation, but today it is illegal to sell elk—or any other wild game—to anyone.

Out-of-towners who trek here for the hunt might prize a bull rack or an elk's "ivory teeth," the highly polished teardrop-shaped canines still collected and traded for decoration as they were for generations by the Nez Perce. But for local hunters, it isn't the mounted heads or skins they covet, but the backstrap, ribs, steaks, and stew meat. A cow can weigh four hundred pounds and a bull over seven hundred, yielding enough to keep a person in daily elk for a year.

When I realized that hunters aren't as willing to share their bounty as gardeners with surplus tomatoes, I bartered with the local ski guide for a piece of his elk. He had given me my first taste of elk on a backcountry ski trip a few years before. One evening by firelight in an old miner's cabin, he cooked chili, thick and tomatoey, filled with kidney beans and green peppers. When I learned the stew meat was elk, this ordinary chili became exotic, perhaps forbidden, transformed by its wildness. It was a difference I could feel, but with all the chili powder, one I couldn't truly taste.

When I brought my sirloin steak home, it looked foreign on the kitchen counter. Deep purple-red, like a beet, it was glossy and startlingly lean. Not only had the fat been trimmed away, but the usual marbling that weaves through the flesh of other meat, rendering it tender and succulent, was simply not there. I searched for clues to tap into its untamed flavors. I feared that the wrong move would tense the muscle fibers like an animal in flight. I found recipes for elk, but they were too much like that chili, smothered in tomato sauce and cream of mushroom soup, safeguards against any hint of the meat's gaminess—the pure, musky taste of wildness. For most, this essence, startlingly exotic and intimate, is too potent to consume. But it is what I wanted to hold in my mouth and savor.

When my hunt through the local library and history museum to find records of how a pioneer woman would have cooked her game proved fruitless, I called Janie Tippett. Janie is a writer, photographer, and rancher's wife who has lived off the land for nearly all of her seventy years. She has horse-packed sourdough starter and fresh milk into the heart of the Wallowa Mountains to cook for elk- and deer-hunting camps. And she is matter-of-fact about ways of life she takes for granted. How to cook a wild animal she has just killed is one of them. "You cook it just like beef," she said when I told her about my steak. "Last six meals we've had elk," she said. Stuffed peppers, meat loaf, minestrone, chicken-fried steak.

A hunter can't talk about cooking elk without talking about how it was killed. "You have to field-dress it quickly, then chill it," Janie said. Elk are so large and so hot, they have to be gutted right where they were shot or the meat will spoil. "When you shoot it, that's when the work starts," she said. This year, Janie held a leg while her husband, Doug, field-dressed it. But she once gutted an elk by herself when she needed the meat to feed herself and her young son.

I imagined her then as she is now, with her open face, long white hair, and agile body, struggling against the bulk of the fresh-killed beast to get at its belly. She poised the wide blade just below the breastbone and eased it under the skin, slicing back to the anus, careful not to burst the intestines, puncture the stomach, or sever the bladder. The first cut released a rush of sweetness, like fresh-mown grass, and the guts spilled out onto the bunchgrass. She lifted out the liver, checking its smell and color to make sure that the elk was healthy, and set it aside for frying and eating fresh. She reached up under the ribs to pull out the lungs and the heart, placing heart next to liver, to let the cavity cool. After all this, she settled into the heavy labor of quartering the elk, letting the knife find the spaces between bone and socket, between ribs. She skinned around the neck to keep the hair out of the meat and cut off the head. She might have cut out the tongue, too, a particular favorite of Teddy Roosevelt, who wrote, "Elk tongues are the most delicious eating, being juicy, tender and well-flavored; they are excellent to take out as a lunch on a long hunting trip." But she had to decide what parts to take and what to leave for the coyotes, ravens, and bears. It was four long trips to the pickup, straining under the weight of each quarter with the help of only a small boy.

The only elk recipe Janie has written down is a treasured, two-century-old family recipe for elk mincemeat made from its long, bulky neck. "It has to be the neck," she said. Like the recipes in nineteenth-century cookbooks, the instructions are based on years' worth of cooking knowledge that for the most part has been lost with the ranchers and farmers who have left the land. "You simmer it on the wood cookstove for a long time until it's cooked," she said. "It's the best mincemeat you'll ever eat."

A week after hunting season ended, I read about Velma Buchanan in the *Chieftain* newspaper. At eighty-four, Velma was butchering her elk when she had a heart attack. The week before, she had shot it from among a herd of seven hundred fleeing at a dead run. Later, I visited her friend and hunting partner, Sallie Tanzey. She told me that Velma was a rancher's wife who could mend fence, pull calves, and tend her garden all on the same day. And she knew how to work her knife through the threads of muscle and sinew, around invisible bones, saving every scrap of meat for eating. "She still had all her own teeth," Sallie said. Velma's skinned elk had hung in the barn for a week to age, and they were cutting steaks and grinding meat together, like they did every year, when Velma's heart stopped.

I asked Sallie to tell me about one of their favorite ways to cook elk. "I have this elk steak . . ." I explained.

"You just cook it," Sallie said.

I looked at her blankly. I was a stranger to Sallie, a fast-talking newcomer, and she was kind but guarded. Suddenly, her face softened and she said, "Come on. Let's cook some." She led me into the kitchen and heated up a cast-iron pan, her descriptions warming up, too. "Elk is a moister meat than deer," she said, unwrapping thin, dark scallopini, dredging them in flour, and putting them in the hot pan with oil and margarine. She moved quickly but not urgently, her slim body and well-used hands natural to the task. "I never saw Velma open a recipe book," she said. "She was a great country cook." Velma, like all the women hunters who have lived and died here, learned to cook as she learned to hunt—without books, perhaps without words.

Tiny puddles of blood pooled on top of the meat slices before Sallie flipped them over. They sizzled and steamed. "It's cubed, so I can cook it a bit faster," she said. She checked it once to make sure it had browned and put it all on a plate for me. Exceptionally tender with a fibery texture, the elk tasted nutty, sweet, and intensely meaty. As I chewed, she told me how she'd make her pan gravy. She told me how to make jerky and stew. She paused, looked at me, and said, "It's worth it after it's said and done. Sometimes I think, 'Why did I shoot it in that draw?' But when it's hanging you think, 'That was a great hunt.'"

On the drive out of the canyon where Sallie lives, snow fell on the dry road and disappeared into the brown bunchgrass. Cows fed on hay in the narrow pastures lodged between stream and canyon wall. Cake tiers of basalt climbed toward clouds to the places where hidden elk were grazing. The remains of the elk Sallie cooked, Velma's last, were in a bag on the passenger seat. It filled the car with its complex aroma like a robust red wine poised under the nose, provocative. I inhaled its sweetness. I thought of the lifetime of clear creek water, cheatgrass, and wild hawthorn reduced to that small mass, of the rituals of hunting and eating, cooking and death. And all the way home, the flavors sang in my throat, like the ululation of a bull elk bugling.

RECIPES

Elk Mincemeat

Janie Tippett's recipe for elk mincemeat has been handed down through four generations along with the lidded wooden container used to store it for long periods of time. Like most early mincemeat recipes, hers contains suet, the solid white fat from the kidneys and loins. Today, Janie omits the suet, but she insists that the meat be wild and prefers the apple cider be home pressed. Following tradition, she bakes it into a double-crust pie for special occasions. *Note*: Her recipe calls for bowls instead of cups. Any size bowl will work, as will a standard measuring cup, provided the same measure is used for each ingredient.

INGREDIENTS:

Elk neck, cut into pieces, enough to make 3 bowls of
  chopped meat
5 bowls chopped apples
1 bowl chopped suet (optional)
3 bowls chopped raisins
1 bowl chopped currants
1 bowl dark corn syrup
1 bowl apple cider vinegar

2 bowls sweet cider
3 bowls granulated sugar
1 tablespoon black pepper
Salt to taste
Cloves to taste
Cinnamon to taste
Nutmeg to taste

Boil the elk neck. Simmer it on the wood cookstove until the meat falls off the bone. Put it through a meat grinder. Cook everything together in a cast-iron Dutch oven. Use less sugar if the cider or the apples are sweet. Simmer it for a long time until it's cooked. Seal the mincemeat in quart jars while it's hot.

Fried Elk Steak with Pan Gravy

An impromptu cooking lesson with Wallowa County native Sallie Tanzey taught me the secrets to keeping this exceptionally lean game steak tender: use ample fat in the pan and cook it quickly. Because she killed, cleaned, and butchered the meat herself, Sallie knew that it was safe to serve when still pink inside, not well-done as the cookbooks cautiously instruct.

INGREDIENTS:

2 tablespoons vegetable oil
3 tablespoons butter or margarine
1 pound elk steaks, about an inch thick
Salt and pepper to taste
1 cup flour
1 cup cold milk

Heat a cast-iron pan over medium-high heat. Pour in the oil and melt 1 tablespoon of the butter or margarine in the pan. Salt and pepper the steaks and dredge them in the flour. Shake off excess. When the butter is bubbling but before it has browned, add the steaks to the pan and sear, cooking until the flour coating has browned, about 4 minutes. Flip and cook another 3 minutes, or until the second side is well browned.

Remove the steaks to a platter and cover to keep warm. Lower the heat to medium and add the remaining 2 tablespoons of butter and 2 tablespoons of the flour to the pan drippings. Stir with a fork or whisk until it has formed a paste. Cook it for one minute more. Whisk in the milk and stir the sauce until it is hot and thickened enough to coat the back of a spoon. Season to taste with salt and pepper. Serve with the elk steaks.

Boiled Fresh Elk Tongue

In *The Works of Theodore Roosevelt* (1893), Roosevelt wrote, "For a steady diet no meat tastes better or is more nourishing than elk venison." He lamented the overhunting of the elk, which once ranged over the entire continental United States. But that didn't stop him from shooting the last bull elk seen near his ranch on the Little Missouri. He might have done it for the tongue, the subject of a rare tasting note among his volumes of hunting stories.

INGREDIENTS:

1 fresh elk tongue, about 2 pounds
2 bay leaves
1 small onion, thinly sliced
1 teaspoon peppercorns
1 teaspoon salt

Place tongue, bay leaves, onion, peppercorns, and salt in a pan and just cover with water. Bring to a simmer and cook for about 2 hours until the tongue is tender and the skin curls back at the root. Cool the tongue in the liquid. When cool, peel off the outer skin, trim the root, and slice it for serving.

Up Your Goose
with a Boneless Duck

CHRIS OFFUTT

There are two kinds of writers, you will hear people say, the ones who drink and the ones who quit. Writers who make money and those who make art. Writers with an agent and writers who want one. Published and unpublished, student and established, commercial and literary. In private, writers distinguish between those who deserve success and those who don't. The first group is always small, confined to the close friends of the person making the judgment. To this endless and ridiculous list, I'd like to add another crucial distinction—writers who cook and writers who don't.

My own path to becoming a cooking writer began in childhood, that refuge of blame and sorrow so many of us put to literary use. I grew up in a town of two hundred in the Appalachian foothills of eastern Kentucky, where many of our neighbors hunted and fished for the table, grew vegetables for canning, and slaughtered hogs in the fall. My father was a noncooking writer of fantasy and pornographic novels. My mother was a lousy cook.

Mom was the eldest daughter of an alcoholic father and a slowly dying mother. She lacked an instructor of culinary skills—no mother, no sister, no aunt—but bore the burden of preparing daily meals as a young teenager. Cooking was a lifelong and thankless drudgery carried out with grim determination.

Contributing to my mother's lack of enthusiasm for the kitchen was the fact that she seldom ate. Dad didn't like fat women, and Mom complied by starving herself. At supper she sat before an empty plate. Every night she watched her family eat meals she forbade herself, then washed all the dishes.

My mother's specialty was a casserole composed of canned vegetables, canned soup, and leftovers, topped with crumbled crackers and processed cheese. The side dishes were vegetables from a can—mushy, wet, and tasteless. Dessert was Jell-O or canned fruit. Occasionally Mom lodged chunks of canned fruit in Jell-O, sometimes mixed with celery. Once a week we ate roast chicken. Depression-raised in a log cabin, my father ate the neck, gizzard, heart, and liver, chewed the gristle from the joints, then split the bones and sucked the dark marrow. This feat of consumption impressed me deeply. I ate as often as possible at our neighbors' houses. They fed me scratch-made biscuits and gravy, fresh sausage, rabbit stew, roast possum, and my favorite meal of squirrel.

I dropped out of high school to join the army, eager for quality food. Unfortunately, I failed the physical and remained in Kentucky another five years. When I finally left, I was extremely skinny, in possession of a horrific and ever-flourishing case of facial acne, and had absolutely no knowledge of a proper diet. I liked to drink and smoke dope. I rarely showered. I suffered migraines. I'd never cooked a single meal.

At age twenty-two I worked as a dishwasher and ate fresh vegetables for the first time. I became a vegetarian immediately. Restaurants were ideal for me because of the short shifts, shelter from weather, free food, and social interaction. My complexion cleared. I also learned a particularly humbling truth—waitresses wouldn't give the time of day to a dishwasher. I began waiting tables, a career move motivated exclusively by the desire for sex. So passed the decade of my twenties, squandered on vegetables, women, literary dreams, and more than twenty restaurant jobs.

Many years later I accepted an offer as a visiting professor of creative writing at the University of Montana. Missoula sits in a valley formed by three clear rivers surrounded by snow-capped mountains, alive with bear and panther. Long winters beget magic summers with daylight lasting until ten at night. Sunsets turn the sky red and the mountains purple.

The Montana writing community is large for such a small town, close-knit, gossipy, and surprisingly supportive of one another's work. Far more importantly—the writers cooked! Everyone gathered frequently for great meals, great conversation, and great flowing tankards of alcohol. I felt as if I'd entered French café society between the wars. For the first time in my life, I had found a place I could fit into. Montana was like Kentucky with bookstores.

I was invited to a grand autumn feast, attended by all the Missoula literary luminaries and showcasing their culinary artistry. As the fabled day fast approached, I was at a loss for what to prepare. The Montana palate is eclectic and all-encompassing—an annual event was the Testicle Festival, featuring Rocky Mountain Oysters harvested from young bulls.

Faced with master chefs and exotic fare, I decided to honor my roots by preparing squirrel. Unfortunately, they require an abundance of nut trees and the rugged Rockies lacked hardwoods in general. Squirrels were scarce, and quite lean from their limited diet. I was forced to substitute.

While a chicken roasted in the oven, I chopped onion, garlic, celery, carrot, potato, and walnut. Everything was diced to perfection, seasoned to enhance the diversity of flavor. I skinned and deboned the chicken, cubed it to tiny increments, and marinated it briefly in a blend of soy, mustard, and tarragon.

Then I assembled the ingredients into a casserole modeled after my mother's meals.

I arrived to a boisterous crowd and three tables jammed with wondrous food—venison, elk, fresh-caught trout, and ostrich. Montana has a short but rich growing season that yields vegetables and herbs, including wild asparagus. Another table held magnificent desserts—homemade huckleberry pie, a triple-layer chocolate cake, and hand-churned ice cream. I presented my casserole to the host and proudly proclaimed it as squirrel.

Writers were everywhere, engaged in typical conversation—complaining about agents, comparing editors, discussing book deals, gauging the season's fishing, confirming that western prose was indeed unappreciated, and complimenting each other's meals. Jon Jackson, author of ten terrific crime novels, brought Game Bird Pie. He also referred to it as Three Birds in the Bush and Up Your Goose with a Boneless Duck. Preparation had been extensive. Jon had acquired a fresh goose and duck, plucked and gutted both, then disarticulated each bird. He made a forcemeat of pheasant, wild leeks, and morels into a loaf, around which he carefully wrapped the duck. Then he inserted the duck into the cavity of the goose. This was carefully placed in a coffin of pastry dough, sealed with a topcoat of dough, and baked in a covered dish. The result was tender enough to be sliced. The pastry dough was flaky yet contained the flavors of wild fowl. Everyone raved about Jon's creation.

Periodically, I checked my chicken casserole, but no one had tried it. I surreptitiously removed a few portions in the hope that people would recognize its popularity and try some. No dice. Apparently word had spread quick as double-triggers that Offutt had brought squirrel. Hunting in Montana was often an expeditionary venture that involved wall tents, pack animals or four-wheelers, and a great deal of powerful munitions. Perhaps an animal you shot with a .22 and carried home in a sack was not a worthy foe. Or maybe the squirrel was regarded as a rodent on par with a rat. All I knew was nobody ate my casserole and my little feelings were hurt.

I resolved to reveal the truth and went to the front porch, where a cluster of senior writers was holding forth with bourbon and cigarettes. David James Duncan had arrived late. Dave is a renowned writer of fiction, lecturer of environmental and spiritual concerns, professional angler, and occasional river guide. He's a good-humored man. As a prank, someone gave him a portion of my dish, waiting until the first bite was in Dave's mouth before telling him it was squirrel. The timing was perfect: just as I stepped onto the porch, Dave spat his entire bite into the darkness of the yard. My appearance created a brief air of concern that I dispelled by laughing, joined heartily by everyone present. I was in with the gang.

The evening continued with a great flood of aperitifs and heavily praised desserts, each of which resembled a baker's advertisement. Just before leaving, I was approached by

James Welch, a writer whose work I deeply admire. Jim's heritage is Blackfeet and Gros Ventre, and he grew up on the Fort Belknap Reservation, where much of his work is set. We had met several years before, while I was in graduate school, when I heard him read. After the reading, Jim joined a few of us unruly young students for a beer. He was the first writer I'd met who wrote about rural people as isolated and oppressed as those in Appalachia. We discussed the difficulties of rendering their reality to readers who knew nothing about life on the rez or in the hills. His advice was succinct: "Show them the world without explaining it."

Now Jim stopped me in the midst of revelry, surrounded by his many longtime friends, and told me that the food I'd brought was good. "I ate squirrel when I was a kid," he said.

The situation felt like a practical joke taken too far. I confessed to Jim that it was actually chicken, and no one else had eaten any. "Don't tell them," I said. He agreed and we laughed a long time together, not as writers or friends, but as a pair of outlanders who'd put one over on town people. Later I concluded that there was no real reason for Jim to revive childhood memory by sampling squirrel as an adult. He was simply the nicest guy at the gathering. He knew the outsider's role and wanted me to feel welcome.

At the end of the academic year, I filled a U-Haul and left Montana with great reluctance. I learned a great deal while I was there—how to fly-fish, play poker, and recognize the signs of recent bear activity. I found community and friends, and a landscape to rival the hills of home. I also discovered another method of dividing writers—those who eat squirrel and those who don't.

RECIPE

Baked Possum

The neighbor man who served me possum died several years ago. He said he'd eaten it during lean times, especially in the Great Depression. He told me that people ate half their yard back then. He'd even tried owl, but there wasn't much meat for as big as it looked and all the noise it made.

The following recipe is from *More than Moonshine: Appalachian Recipes and Recollections,* by Sydney Saylor Farr. She includes this caveat before the recipe: "Possum meat is strong but gamey, and elaborate methods of cooking had to be used to make it palatable."

INGREDIENTS:

1 dressed possum
1 tablespoon butter
1 large onion

1 cup breadcrumbs
1/2 teaspoon chopped red pepper
Dash of steak sauce
1 hard-boiled egg, chopped
Salt to taste
Small amount of water
1 or 2 sprigs of sassafras root

Dress the possum or have it done for you.

For the stuffing: Melt butter in frying pan and add onion. When onion begins to brown, add chopped liver of possum and cook until tender and well-done. Add bread-crumbs, red pepper, steak sauce, egg, salt, and water to moisten mixture.

Stuff the possum with the mixture and sew up the opening. Put in a roasting pan, add 2 tablespoons water, and roast in moderate oven (300–350 degrees) until meat is very tender and a golden brown. Baste the possum frequently in its own fat. When it is done, take from the oven, remove stitches, and put possum on a hot platter. Skim the grease from the drippings and serve gravy in a separate dish.

To add flavor, slip a sprig or two of sassafras root down into the stuffing between the stitches after you have sewn the possum up.

Serve the possum with baked sweet potatoes and green vegetables along with cornbread and coffee or milk.

The Taste of a Wild Mushroom

EUGENIA BONE

I have recently made the transition from lousy mushroomer to successful mushroomer. This has opened many doors for me: culinary, romantic, and spiritual. In fact, the mushroom has become the most symbolic vegetable in my life. There even seems to be a relationship between fungi and men I have loved, and both are intricately tied to a certain kind of longing.

My seminal mushroom experience embodies that longing. When you want something to happen badly enough and then it does, it almost seems as if you have created a sort of magic. When I was young, I lived with my parents and siblings on a hobby farm in Westchester, New York. One spring day—Sunday, I think, because there was no school—my father was very upset about something and I felt terrible for him. Frightened, too. I longed to make him feel better. My father, Edward Giobbi, is a celebrated cook, and food has always been his joy, particularly the discovery of wild edibles. So I went in search of a morel mushroom, which I believed would cheer him up. I looked for the mushroom the same way a diviner looks for water. Not with willow wands, but with an intuition that came easier back then, when I was a child and still more a thing of nature than a product of culture. I walked without pause to an old rotting apple tree—nowhere else—and dropped my eyes down to the large morel, brown and brainy, fleshy and slick as a pampered young man, that awaited me. I longed, and something I longed for happened.

My father was very impressed with the mushroom. And that's all I remember. Unfortunately, morels (*Morchella esculenta*) are elusive, and I never again found one under the rotting apple tree. Eventually, the tree was cut down and its stump removed, and my mother planted zinnias in its place. As I grew older and sharpened my personal likes and dislikes, my connection to mushrooms grew apace. On my nineteenth birthday, a friend of my father's, the former *Gourmet* critic Jay Jacobs, a petite shiitake of a man, took me to lunch at Felidia, in New York, where we ate the caps of porcini mushrooms grilled and dressed with olive oil. (Okay, it was a novelty in

1979.) I thought it was the most sumptuous thing I'd ever eaten: rich, light, perfumey. It sealed my passion for fungi. But while I ate many kilos of mushrooms here and abroad, I did not find another truly great specimen like my father's morel for the next twenty years. The truth is, my longings turned toward more citified rewards, and I began to doubt the wisdom of gathering wild mushrooms at all.

I knew from childhood what the genus *Amanita* was: the Death Cap, *Amanita phalloides*; the Destroying Angels, *Amanita bisporigera* and *Amanita virosa*—the pristine white mushrooms that felled caesars and popes and elephant kings. When eaten, within six to twenty-four hours Amanita induces severe vomiting, abdominal pain, and diarrhea, then jaundice, kidney failure, liver deterioration, and convulsions. Finally, in a matter of days, death. But not all poisonous mushrooms are *that* poisonous: most will just make you sick. The old wives' tale that warns against eating little brown mushrooms is probably a good one to remember, as lots of little brown varieties will give you a stomachache. Some mushrooms are so slightly poisonous, they don't even affect everyone. We used to buy Christmas trees from an old Italian, Nick, who often ate a mushroom that my dad thought was poisonous. Nick said they were delicious. "But it's strange," he'd say, "after eating them, I always fall asleep." And then there is the bit of poison in psychoactive mushrooms that affects the central nervous system. Many times I've seen the *Amanita muscaria*, also known as fly agaric, in the Colorado mountains. Lectures on this and other mushrooms with psychoactive properties are particularly well attended at the annual Telluride mushroom festival.

In time, I was not sure I could even identify a morel anymore. But I rediscovered that miraculous feeling of materializing my desires on duck hunts, waiting in the cathedrals of flooded woods for a mallard drake and hen to alight; waiting, in breathless hush. The act of yearning for birds to descend from the sky sharpens the senses. Only in that heightened state am I capable of feeling the change in the air before a duck flutters into my sights. I learned, early on, that without desire I would never see a duck soon enough to shoot it. It was as a bird hunter, then, that I went to Tuscany to hunt truffles with my second cousin Mario. Mario used to hunt birds and the small Italian boar, the *cingale*, but restrictions on the sport pushed him toward this significantly more profitable activity.

I remember my parents eating truffles grated over pasta in trattorias in Florence, but I'd never eaten them myself. I suppose they are the ultimate fungi. Certainly, throughout history it seems this has been so. Jacob ordered his wife Leah to find them for him, and only a little later (2600 BC) Pharaoh Caeb's chefs were using truffles in the palace kitchens. Pythagoras, Cicero, Plutarch, and Pliny the Elder all wrote about the truffle, which was prepared in Roman times as a salad, sliced raw and dressed with pepper, coriander, oil, and honey. Mario hunts them with an ugly little canine called a Lagotto. As we scrambled after his dog through the underbrush, our noses on the alert for that indescribable yet devastatingly strong smell, I experienced the same connection to nature that I do when hunting birds—longing combined with alertness, which is a state of mind that allows for marvelous things to happen.

We did find truffles, the *Tuber magnatum Pico*, also known as the Alba. Maria, Mario's wife, ground one up with sweet butter and spread the paste over salty crackers, and others she used in a pasta dish with egg yolks and mascarpone cheese. I don't bother eating Picos in the United States because they rarely survive the trip overseas, but I do like truffle butter, which I spread on top of grilled T-bones and lamb chops, and truffle oil to excite savory salads. Truffles are not found in Colorado, where I have property—yet. This fall, though, maybe I will channel my longing. Such conjuring has worked before.

After the truffle hunt, I was ready to become reacquainted with my inner mycologist. I bought books like *Mushrooms of Colorado* and *The Encyclopedia of Food* that told me mushrooms, the fruiting body of a fungus, are about 90 percent water (like us); that they are organized by genus and species, by families, orders, classes, and subdivisions; and that they are all in the kingdom of Fungi. I learned fungi don't make their own food but must get it from an outside host, and that they produce spores, not seeds. It's kind of creepy how much like an animal mushrooms really are. But reading is not the same thing as eating, and I knew the only way I was going to learn was if I had a teacher.

Mushrooming for the table is, ultimately, an oral tradition. I needed someone to show me edible mushrooms growing in their habitat. I needed to experience the terrain and weather they preferred.

We have a place in Colorado because my husband is one of those hiking people. His first Christmas gift to me was a sleeping bag. But I couldn't understand the attraction of clambering over scree only to reach the top. I recognize that other people find this immensely rewarding, but I have always connected to nature via food. I never really felt much of a need to find my place in the circle of life any other way. Then I met blond-haired and blue-eyed Peggy Tomaski, masseuse and mycologist, a woman who appealed to me because she is gentle yet shrewd, passionate, and wise. Peggy took me under her wing and into the dark piney woods of the nearby Uncompahgre Plateau.

We walked about, and I wished to find a mushroom Peggy could identify for me. And she wished, too, because we were new friends, and there was potential that we could be good friends, and the granting of our wishes would be a positive omen. It was the beginning of August, early in the season, almost too early to find anything, and as we tromped through the woods I felt the undercurrent of potential disappointment, that the magic would be lost, our newfound kinship would lose momentum, and we would, as a result, settle for a casual acquaintance. But Peggy can conjure, too. With a cry of delight, she found one perfect *Boletus edulis*, also known as the porcini, Steinpilz, or cèpe: fat-stemmed and fat-headed, with a shiny brown cap and no gills. We continued, giddy, instantly bonded, and suddenly there were mushrooms everywhere. She pointed out *Cantharellus cibarius*, chanterelles, the same bright golden yellow as Peggy's head; and *Lactarius deliciosus*, the delicious milky cap, which has orange gills that bleed first red, then green, when you cut them with your thumbnail. We found about two pounds of chanterelles that day, and once home we sautéed them with butter. We rolled up the slick, fleshy nubbits of mushroom in delicate crepes with *queso añejo*, sweet and sour as the milk burp of a baby.

A few weeks later, I reluctantly agreed to a hike up Bald Mountain. We had company, and company expect to climb mountains when they're visiting Colorado. Kevin, as always, was way ahead of me. I trudged up the trail in a grumpy fog—ponderosa pines to my left and right, so what? —and almost bumped into him. He was standing astride a mushroom with a cap as big as a salad plate and a fat, fat stem. "Here's something for you," he said mildly, and plucked it from the earth and gave it to me. It was something, something very special. A king boletus, royalty of mushrooms. And there, and there . . . within a half hour I had filled my backpack. A few had bites missing from where a deer had paused; others were old, their spongy undercaps yellowing, and so we left them to drop their spores in peace. After gathering as much as I had space for, I returned down the trail to wait by the car, poring over each individual in the hoard, until the rest of our party had reached the summit they had come to scale. Once home, we divvied up our haul. Some of the big caps we grilled on the fire with a few slabs of eggplant, and I ground the two together with garlic and salt and lemon juice and dressed it with truffle oil. We dipped big tortilla chips into this lewdly earthy dip, drank cold beer, and marveled. We sliced up the rest of the caps and cooked them with farfalle and chicken broth and lemon zest, then threw all the stems in a robust oxtail-and-hominy soup.

Since then, I have found tidy rows of boletus at ten thousand feet. I have gathered delicious milky caps along a stream ruled by a pair of mink and watched chanterelles emerge through tender pine needles between patches of rain. We have collected hawk's wings (*Sarcodon imbricatus*) and hedgehogs (*Hydnum repandum*), and once Kevin found a three-kilo giant western puffball, or *Calvatia booniana*, which we cubed and scrambled with eggs. It tasted like a bland marshmallow. And so my husband's desire has come true. I now enthusiastically hike with him. But while he forges ahead, his long strides covering the miles, head high, breathing the view, I walk in small circles, head down, and check the foot of every tree.

Mushrooming has not only been good for my marriage. It has also helped me better understand my father and, even more important, one of the lessons of old age—that living in the moment is the greatest living of all. For years my father tried unsuccessfully to identify a mushroom that grew near his root cellar in Westchester. I remember the kitchen reeking of compost as he conducted spore tests on the dinner table. Often, at meals with chefs, he would ask them about this mysterious mushroom, and they would grunt in French and shrug. Poor Dad: it seemed this mushroom would never pass from his yard into the culinary realm. Finally, after we, his children, had grown up and were conducting lives of our own, he decided to taste it: to realize it, I think. He chopped some of the mushrooms up, sautéed them with garlic and olive oil, and garnished them with parsley from his garden. He tasted them in the morning, so he could get to the doctor during daylight if he needed to, and they tasted very good. Then he tasted them again the next day. They did not kill him. In fact, this mystery species was the honey mushroom, *Armillaria ostoyae*—not an incredibly choice species, but a precious one to him. It was the mushroom he had eaten as a child; the mushroom he remembered one day when he was pinned facedown in the earth by Nazi gunfire; the mushroom that his father had picked sixty years before and cooked with rabbit and rosemary and wine.

When I first heard this story I thought my dad was nuts. Now I appreciate the fact that he has reached a state of mind where life boils down to the taste of a wild mushroom. And indeed, I long for an old age as wise.

RECIPES

Rabbit with Mushrooms

This is an adaptation of a recipe that was first published in my father's book *Pleasures of the Good Earth* (Knopf, 1991). It was my grandfather's recipe. He used the honey mushroom that my father finally rediscovered after decades of remembering. This recipe calls for elephant beans, a Greek import that is notoriously difficult to find. You can omit them, or you can call the International Grocery, at 543 Ninth Avenue between Fortieth and Forty-first Streets in New York City, (212) 279-1000.

serves 4

INGREDIENTS:

1 rabbit (about 3 pounds), cut into serving pieces
Salt and freshly ground black pepper to taste
1 tablespoon chopped fresh rosemary
3 tablespoons olive oil
3 whole cloves garlic, unpeeled
3 cups wild mushrooms, sliced
1 cup dry white wine
1 cup peeled, seeded, and chopped tomatoes
1 1/2 cups elephant beans that have been soaked overnight
    and boiled in salted water until tender

Season all the rabbit pieces with salt and pepper. In a well-ventilated space, heat a large iron skillet over medium heat until it is very hot. Add the rabbit pieces and sprinkle with rosemary. Sear the rabbit, turning often, until it begins to brown. This produces a lot of smoke. It's okay—the rabbit won't stick. Add the olive oil and garlic and continue cooking until the rabbit is golden brown all over. Add the mushrooms and wine, cover, and lower the heat. Simmer until the wine reduces to about half the volume (it will look more like gravy than wine). Add the tomatoes, cover, and continue simmering for about 30 minutes. Add the cooked beans and continue cooking for another 15 minutes, stirring occasionally. Let the rabbit stand for 15 minutes before serving.

I like to serve this dish with a stew of bitter greens like rape, brussels sprouts, and escarole cooked with garlic and hot pepper.

Oxtail Soup with Porcini Mushrooms

The oxtail soup recipe below is adapted from an old *Joy of Cooking* (1956). The idea to add wild mushrooms comes from an oxtail soup with chanterelles that I had at a terrific little French joint called Soupçon in Crested Butte, Colorado.

serves 4

INGREDIENTS:

1 ½ pounds disjointed oxtail

1 cup onion, sliced (1 large onion)

2 tablespoons butter

1 teaspoon salt

4 peppercorns

10 cups water

¼ cup parsley, chopped

¼ cup celery, chopped (1 small stalk)

¼ cup carrots, chopped (1 carrot)

¼ cup tomatoes, chopped (1 small tomato)

1 bay leaf

1 tablespoon fresh marjoram (or 1 teaspoon dried)

3 tablespoons butter

2 tablespoons flour

2 cups fresh porcini or other wild mushrooms, sliced

½ cup hominy, cooked according to the instructions on
the bag, or 1 8-ounce can, drained

¼ cup red wine

Place the oxtails, onion, and butter in a deep soup pot and brown over medium heat, about 10 minutes. Add the salt, peppercorns, and water. Cover, and simmer over low heat for 4 hours.

Add the parsley, celery, carrots, tomatoes, bay leaf, and marjoram and continue simmering over medium low heat for another ½ hour. (If the soup has reduced by half, it's reducing too fast, and you should add another 2 cups of water.)

Strain the soup, chill, and skim off the fat. Reheat the soup. Melt 2 tablespoons of butter in a small saucepan over medium heat. Add the flour and stir until the mixture is creamy and begins to yellow. Add about ¼ cup of the broth and cook, stirring, until the broth is dissolved. Add the flour/butter mixture to the soup pot. Heat the remaining tablespoon of butter in a small skillet over medium heat. Add the mushrooms to the soup and sauté them until their water cooks out, about 15 minutes. Remove and chop the mushrooms into pieces. Add the cooked hominy, the wine, and the mushrooms and heat thoroughly.

Farfalle with Wild Mushrooms

The day we found ten pounds of king boletus in the West Elk mountains, my brother Cham prepared this dish. It is one of the best recipes I've had for bringing out the delicate flavor of wild mushrooms.

serves 4 as an entrée, 6 as a first course

INGREDIENTS:

4 tablespoons olive oil

1 large onion, finely chopped (about 2 cups)

2 garlic cloves, minced

1 lb (6 cups) mixed wild mushrooms cut into 2-inch chunks and slices

1/4 teaspoon soy sauce

1/4 teaspoon sugar

1/4 teaspoon salt

1 1/4 cup chicken broth

1 pound farfalle or other flat pasta, such as fettuccine or pappardelle

1 tablespoon lemon juice (about 1/2 medium lemon)

2 teaspoons lemon zest

3 tablespoons butter

1 1/2 cups grated Parmesan cheese

3 tablespoons lemon basil (or regular basil), finely chopped

Heat the oil in a large nonstick skillet over medium heat. Add the onion and garlic and cook until the onion becomes translucent, about 5 minutes. Add the mushrooms and cook until the liquid cooks out, about 15 minutes. Stir in the soy, sugar, and salt. Set aside.

Place the chicken broth in a small saucepan and warm over medium heat. Bring a large pot of salted water to a boil. Add the pasta and cook until al dente, about 12 minutes. Drain and add to the mushrooms. Add the warm chicken stock, lemon juice, zest, and butter. Toss, cooking over medium heat until the pasta is saturated by the chicken broth, about 5 minutes. Garnish with grated cheese and lemon basil.

Chanterelle Crêpes

On the Western Slope, chanterelles come in about the same time as the pheasant and chukar season starts, so we like to serve these crêpes beside roasted wild birds. You can use any crepe recipe, but I like this uncomplicated one from the *Joy of Cooking* (1959).

makes about 12 crêpes

INGREDIENTS:

The Mushroom Filling

2 tablespoons butter
1 cup onion, chopped (1 large onion)

4 cups fresh chanterelles or other wild mushrooms,
  sliced (about 2 pounds)
½ teaspoon salt
½ teaspoon soy sauce
½ teaspoon sugar
2 cups *queso añejo* or dried ricotta cheese, crumbled

Heat the butter in a large nonstick pan over moderate heat. Add the onion and cook until it becomes translucent, about 5 minutes. Add the mushrooms and cook until the liquid cooks out, about 15 minutes. Add the salt, soy, and sugar. Remove from heat and transfer to a bowl. Add 1 cup of the crumbled cheese and carefully mix.

The Crêpes

¾ cup flour
½ teaspoon salt
1 teaspoon baking powder
2 eggs, beaten
⅔ cup milk
⅓ cup water
3-tablespoon lump of butter

Combine the dry ingredients in a bowl. In a separate bowl, combine the wet ingredients. Add the wet ingredients to the dry ingredients and mix with a few strokes. Don't worry about the lumps. Place in the refrigerator for half an hour.

Heat a small nonstick skillet over medium heat. Rub the interior with the lump of butter. Add 1 large cooking-spoonful of batter. Tip the skillet so the batter spreads evenly all over the bottom of the pan. Cook the crêpe over moderate heat for about 3 minutes, until the edges look dry, then, with a spatula, flip the crêpe over and cook another 30 seconds to 1 minute. Lay the crêpe on a piece of wax paper. Cover with another piece of wax paper.

Continue this process until all the batter is used up. *Note*: If you hate flipping crêpe, then just cook them on one side a little bit longer. They'll taste and look just as good.

To Assemble the Crêpes

Preheat oven to 400 degrees.

Place one crêpe on a clean counter or surface. Place about 3 tablespoons of the mushroom mixture on the lower third of the crêpe. Roll the crêpe up and place it in a casserole pan about 8 x 12 inches. Continue doing this until you have filled up the pan (you may need a second pan). Distribute the remaining cheese evenly over the crêpes.

Place in the hot oven and cook until the cheese melts and the mushrooms heat through, about 10 minutes.

Eggplant and Porcini Dip

makes 2 cups

INGREDIENTS:

4 slices eggplant, about 1 inch thick
4 slices porcini mushroom, about 1 inch thick
4 garlic cloves
½ cup olive oil
4 tablespoons lemon juice (about 1 lemon)
Salt and freshly ground black pepper to taste
1 tablespoon coriander, finely chopped
Truffle oil for garnish (optional)

The best way to prepare the eggplant and mushrooms is to grill them over fire. Just place them on a hot grill and cook 3 to 5 minutes on the first side, turn over, and grill 3 minutes on the second side. If a grill is not available, place the eggplant and mushroom slices on a cookie tray and broil until they brown, 3 to 5 minutes, then, with a spatula, turn them over and continue broiling another 3 minutes, until they begin to brown.

Place the eggplant, mushrooms, garlic, olive oil, and lemon juice in a food processor or blender. Process until blended but not to a smooth paste (a few little chunks are good). Transfer to a serving bowl and add salt and pepper to taste. Sprinkle with coriander and a dribble of truffle oil, if you like. Serve warm or at room temperature with tortilla chips or smeared on top of crostini.

The End of Laughter

LAN SAMANTHA CHANG

How can I tell the story of our love affair that never took place? There are no words for it. It was not a liaison, a dalliance, or a fling. It was not friendship and not family. It's an attachment, I would say to you. An attachment with no usefulness in real life.

It happened in a city on a faraway coast. In that hilled city, winter shadows lengthened early, and so our attachment flourished in the dark. Our darkness was not frightening or cold. Our darkness gleamed with happiness; it was sustaining;

it wrapped around us like a curtain and kept us safe from gossip. You were beautiful and I was old, and we were both with other people. We were not allowed to touch. We never held hands. We never made love and so, instead, we ate.

We ate hamburgers and sushi and pancakes with pecans. We ate chicken fingers, tapenades, French chocolates, and ice cream shakes. To carve out time, we had late lunches, early dinners, and frequent duplicate meals, reassuring each other that we had not eaten recently and could use a bite. We ate for love, for sympathy and fun. We ate out of confusion and emptiness and lust. We ate our meals in public and kept our true hungers a secret.

Although you could not come to Hangzhou, your letters followed me there, and I wrote back to you about the beggars' chicken and crisp fish. You flew home to Boston for two weeks, surfacing after an eternity with tales of Portuguese tapas and stuffy family recipes. Together we visited the cuisine of China, Japan, and Thailand; over lunch we went to Pakistan, Ethiopia, and France. We traveled far in search of our meals. We snuck off in the middle of the day and drove to the wine country. We ordered too much and sat in restaurants for hours. And at those meals we never discussed the people nearby. We never chatted with the waiters and we never paid attention to the silverware, the dishes, the artwork, or the atmosphere. I don't remember the names of the places where we went. I don't remember the prices. I remember laughing on the street, winter rain in your brown hair. I remember watching the dark descend: soon it would be dinnertime.

I remember a diner where we always ordered breakfast no matter what the time of day. Breakfast offered solace and helped us ignore the clock. We let the time slide by and chatted over our French toast. We stayed an extra half hour and then another half hour, trifling the time away because it was our enemy.

I remember a dim cave, the recessed tunnel of a Greek restaurant where no one ever came. Steam from our hot potatoes fogged the window. You told me how alone you felt and how you couldn't sleep. You envied my forthcoming book, my answered questions. We were more than years apart, you said; our age difference put us into different times of life. That evening you were frightened, unsure of whom you would become and whether you would ever satisfy your dreams. I said that you were like my college friend Peter, who was always valiant, largehearted, and ambitious. I didn't tell you Peter had been ill and died when you were twelve years old. Instead, I said you would never be alone and I'd be there for you. In my heart I knew this wasn't true, that someday you would love someone appropriate and I would not forgive you. I said it because I wished it. As I wished the winter would never go away.

I remember a Chinese restaurant high on a hill. You felt we should celebrate the arrival of spring. I dreaded the coming of long days, but didn't want to tell you, so we ordered dumplings swimming in a spicy sauce, scallion pancakes, the stir-fried special vegetable, "eight delights" chow fun, twin lobsters with ginger, salted rock crab with hot peppers, and steamed sea bass with soy sauce. The waitress said we'd ordered too much. We set out to prove her wrong.

We split the pancakes evenly. They were delicious, loaded with scallions sliced leaf-thin. The special vegetable was *kong xin cai*, a Chinese staple with a hollow stem. I translated its name for you: "hollow-hearted green." You went at the steaming *kong xin cai* with a voluptuous greed that made me look away. I saw then, coming toward us, the enormous platter of chow fun, bulging with brilliant greens and curved pink shrimp and waving tentacles among its eight delights, including one unidentifiable delight you later claimed was tripe. I felt I'd had enough to eat when the three seafood plates turned up. You kept on, deliberately and with confidence; your capacity for everything was prodigious.

I watched you dismember sea creatures, something you had learned to do when you were growing up and spent your summers on the shore. I watched the oil gleam on your lips; I watched your hands. You had sturdy, homely hands, intelligent and versatile. They had fixed motorcycles and built bookshelves; they had cleaned fish and sharpened a thousand pencils. I laughed at your attempts to get the last of the meat out of the lobster claws, and again at your interest in the vivid, knob-eyed lobster heads, which, you concluded after close

examination, were "cartilaginous" and "merely ornamental."
You kept prying at them, though, unwilling to concede to the
inedible.

In his apartment thirty miles south, my lover ate leftovers
from the beef stew I'd made the day before. At least three girls
were thinking of you that night; you didn't check your phone.
Instead, we talked about the meals we'd had and the meal we
were eating and the meals that were to come. A few times
you stole my water glass. You smiled slyly, put your beautiful
mouth against the glass, and drank. I had slowed down long
ago, but you tried to keep me eating. With your long arms, you
snuck more fish onto my plate.

I said, "I will remember . . ."

And you said, "I will remember . . ."

Staggering down the hill, after having eaten so much that
we could hardly breathe, you told me a story about consuming
birdseed as a child. You had been drawn to it, you explained
to me, because it was forbidden. Then you stopped walking.
I smiled, waiting for you to recognize the irony in what you
had said, but you stood, puzzled, as if struggling to know who
we were and how we had come to this place. Your confusion
only worsened when we both began to giggle. Then I was
snorting and you howled at me because I couldn't stop. We
laughed until our stomachs hurt, until we had no idea why
we'd begun. We were delirious and confused, pickled on too
much dinner.

Afterward, I wondered why giving in to laughter feels so risky. It's because laughter suspends time, you said. When we fall into such giddiness we don't know when it's going to end; when we begin to laugh we step out of time. I told you what my mother believed: that if we laugh too hard we'll cry; and you recalled that as a child, after a long spell of hilarity, you would feel a sudden melancholy. Such as after making love, I said, and you were silent.

You would leave me soon, I knew. The old know what the young do not, and most of all they can foresee the end of youth. I had tried to tell you this, but you refused to hear it. You didn't understand for months, not until you tried to walk away and recognized, too late, that you had ingested me too utterly and too faithfully. I had become a part of you. And then our age difference became embarrassing to you, and our attachment an awkwardness. You grew desperate to cast me off. You shouted; you sobbed; you pushed me away and then called begging to hear my voice. You stormed out of a restaurant and then insisted that you could not live without me. Finally you succeeded. As the days lengthened into midsummer, you spent hours in the pool and refused to eat anything except steamed vegetables and broiled meat. You managed to escape in search of someone more appropriate, someone whose love would not keep you from your glorious dreams.

Now, I recall the words of Graham Greene: "You don't weep unless you've been happy first; tears always mean something enviable." I am aware of what I did. I came to the time in life when we must close the door of a place to which we cannot return. Willfully, I refused to close the door. I laughed too much and stayed too long; so I deserved your punishment. Now I have a husband and a house. You live a thousand miles away. You keep company with women your age or younger, bartenders and poets and consultants and reporters; you don't want to be with anyone for very long. You still dream about the future and taste everything with impunity. There is no need to know that one day you, too, will pass that imperceptible moment after which you begin to dream of the past. Perhaps then you will remember the time when you and I used to walk into a restaurant filled with hunger and the yearning to be fed.

RECIPE

Hollow-Hearted Greens

INGREDIENTS:

A big bunch of *kong xin cai* (sold in Chinese grocery stores)
Garlic
Vegetable oil, corn oil, or peanut oil (I use corn oil)
Salt

Prep: Dice at least one clove of garlic and wash the *kong xin cai*. Trim off a portion of the hollow stems. Remember that when they hit the oil the leaves must be dry, or else the dish will be watery.

Stir-fry: Heat three tablespoons of oil in a pan. Wait patiently until the slightest moisture on its surface will strike back at you. Throw in the garlic. Then, when the garlic turns pale yellow, throw in the *kong xin cai*. Stir-fry quickly, so that the leaves are just glazed with oil. Sprinkle in the salt and stir-fry until the leaves have shriveled and turned dark green. Serve immediately.

In a Crowded Kitchen

A CULINARY AND LITERARY PORTRAIT OF GUILLAUME APOLLINAIRE

HEATHER HARTLEY

Hors d'oeuvres cubistes, orphistes, futuristes, etc.
Poisson de l'ami Méritarte
Zone de contrefilet à la Croniamental
Acrelin de chapon à l'Hérésiarque
Méditations esthétiques en salade
Fromages en cortège d'Orphée
Fruits du Festin d'Ésope
Biscuits du Brigadier masqué
Vin blanc de l'Enchanteur
Vin rouge de la Case d'Armons
Champagne des Artilleurs
Café des Soirées de Paris
Alcools

In 1916, two years before the death of French poet Guillaume Apollinaire, his friends honored him with a lavish banquet in Paris—over eighty guests attended, including Picasso, poet Max Jacob, and Cubist painter Juan Gris, who served as emcee. Such sumptuous, voluptuous banquets were very popular in Paris up until the 1920s—any old excuse for a party would do. Undernourished, zealous poets, painters, sculptors, and various bohemians could fête their friends (or acquaintances or enemies) and eat a lot of marvelous food. And Apollinaire's banquet was no different—except that each course cleverly referred to one of his poetry books or other writings, combining some of his most famous works with capons, cookies, and champagne into an appetizing Modernist mélange.

The sizable banquet menu, common in Paris at the turn of the century, showcased traditional French fare, original variations on it, and the sheer volume of good food available in Paris in the '20s. The feeding frenzy may have been in reaction to the Commune of Paris of 1871 when, after the French defeat in the Franco-Prussian War, a bloody civil uprising took place in the capital. During the brief, chaotic rule of the socialist, reformist government that followed, Parisians were forced to eat horse, rat, bear, donkey, dog, and cat, according to Romantic poet Victor Hugo. No wonder Apollinaire and his contemporaries were inventing Cubist appetizers and Orphic cheese courses.

~~~~~~~~~~~~~~~~~~~~~~~~~~~~~

His gourmandise was incredible. Apollinaire would feast upon meats, bread, wine and bouillon and then he would sit down to work until late in the evening.

— Francis Carco, poet and friend

A seminal figure in the Modernist movement, Apollinaire was involved in many avant-garde groups, including Naïve art, Fauvism, Cubism, and Futurism. He is also credited with inventing the word *surrealism*. With such a significant place in the modern literary world, it's curious that little has been written about his obsession with food and drink. Yet an obsession it was: in magazines, newspapers, books, and plays he often wrote about his favorite foods: seafood, fowl, pot-au-feu, stew, risotto, *sanguins* (a rich orange-colored mushroom found in the south of

France), Corsican sausage (in Apollinaire's words, "C'est là une charcuterie de l'Olympe"), oranges, grapes, apples, and sweets of all sorts—he ate just about everything but raw red meat. He was clearly not fussy about regional French foods. Nor was he a culinary chauvinist; in addition to traditional French cooking, he enjoyed Hungarian, Spanish, Chinese, Italian, Greek, Turkish, and African cuisine. And Apollinaire wrote about them all.

His recipes for dishes like omelet with sea urchins and *blaff de maquereaux* (a mysterious mackerel entrée) can be found in numerous issues of the magazine *Mercure de France*, while the erotic novel *Les onze mille verges: or, The amorous adventures of Prince Mony Vibescu* is a cornucopia of sexy fruits. In his book *The Heresiarch and Co.*, Apollinaire wrote about the pungent smells of street markets in the south of France, where he spent his childhood: "The old part of Nice was filled with the odor of fruits and herbs and spices mixed with raw meat, . . . cod and toilets." Introverted gourmands could turn to the "Small Modern Magical Recipes" chapter of *The Poet Assassinated*, which includes an original recipe: *eau-de-vie pour bien parler*. His verse play *Le Marchand d'anchois*, written in collaboration with André Salmon, includes the savory lines "The anchovy invigorates sex / It's exciting, night and day, / There are no bones and it's soft." (Who thought an anchovy could be so arousing? I've always prudishly picked them out of my *salade niçoise*.) Apollinaire was a serious connoisseur and a vociferous critic. His friends knew him as a gourmand. He could also be a real pig.

~~~~~~~~~~~~~~~~~~~~~~~~~~~~~~

Et tu bois cet alcool brûlant comme ta vie
Ta vie que tu bois comme une eau-de-vie
                              —Guillaume Apollinaire

Le Crucifix, Cardinal, Téléphone, Zut, Balzar, Onimus, La Closerie des Lilas—these bars were just a few of Apollinaire's preferred haunts. The aperitif hour almost always united the poet and his friends, often in Montmartre or Montparnasse. "I've been very drunk lately," Apollinaire wrote to a friend in 1904. (Actually, this line could have been written anywhere from 1900 to 1918, as Apollinaire loved to toast friends and lovers and himself.) Some of the most potent drinks he imbibed on a regular basis were *cocktails carabinés*, or raging cocktails— invented by some well-lubricated Norwegian friends. The drinks were a decoction of meat in stout or port, absinthe grog with either lemon juice or a dash of juniper-berry liqueur, and some uncertain ingredient called "advokaat." *Cocktail carabiné* or not, much of what he drank was strong enough to level the portliest of poets. Apollinaire's short list included: vermouth, beer, Rhine wines, absinthe (or *l'herbe sainte* according to Verlaine), and *chartreuse verte* (a little number that included a pinch of crushed snakeskin). The possible etymological origins of one special libation, called *vespétro*, tickled Apollinaire pink: One source says *vespétro* derives from the French verb *vesser*, literally meaning "to fart" or "to burp." A more demure version states that the word is of Latinate origin, *vesper,* or "evening"—therefore a liqueur to drink after an evening meal. Whatever its origin, one must make advance reservations with *vespétro*: the recipe calls for a seven-day maceration period. Ingredients include, among other things, angelica, fennel, coriander, a liter of eau-de-vie, and a lot of sugar. Aperitifs, *cocktails carabinés,* and digestifs were an integral part of Apollinaire's daily habits—so much so that in 1913, he titled one of his most famous poetry collections after this idée fixe: *Alcools.*

~~~~~~~~~~~~~~~~~~~~~~~~~~~~

He had this robust stoutness that gave him a lot of authority. Gourmand, huge, appetizing to look at, he looked like some hilarious god. . . . The more he ate, the more a physical cheerfulness radiated all through him.

—Carco

The significance of Apollinaire's *l'embonpoint,* or stoutness, cannot be overlooked. Being overweight was chic: paunch meant prosperity. French adjectives abound to describe fashionable flab: *bien enrobé, rondeurs exquises, grassouillettes, dodu, potelé, cossu, ventripotent.* Fat sounds infinitely more elegant in French than in English. (Compare, for example, *l'embonpoint* to "lard ass.") Though Apollinaire did not have a lot of money to eat, he had a doting, dominating mother and many friends who all made sure he was well fed. A literary critic once wrote approvingly to Apollinaire, "You live on rue Gros and it suits you well!" During the Belle Époque, your morning coat may have been worn thin, but as long as your love handles were bursting through your buttons, you could surely be numbered among the elite crowd.

~~~~~~~~~~~~~~~~~~~~~~~~~~~~~~~

> The kitchen was a very small room lit by a skylight, with a nasty little table, wobbly chairs and chipped plates. When Apollinaire stood there, one would think that you were in a king's palace. He would smoke, all red and smiling, happy and proud. He was going to eat. . . . You could only see his joy, his smile and his appetite.
>
> —Philippe Soupault, poet and admirer of Apollinaire

Apollinaire's kitchen on boulevard Saint-Germain was a sort of *cuisine-cabinet-de-toilette* complete with bathtub, sink, a small range with two gas plaques, and a blue-green enamel oven. In this humble apartment (which Apollinaire called his *pigeonnier,* or pigeon roost), friends like Picasso, Max Jacob, André Salmon, and Ambroise Vollard would frequently come over for lunch or dinner. To create his meals, Apollinaire spent a lot of time haunting secondhand bookstores and the Bibliothèque nationale in search of fresh recipes. He pestered Parisian chefs and hostesses for the secret ingredients of his favorite dishes, discussed recipes with his friends, made suggestions, remarked on faults, and debated his dinners down to the last grain of salt. Once, at a dinner party, he went so far as to bar everyone from the kitchen so that his hostess could focus all of her gracious hospitality on the perfect lobster. His personal book collection included *La Cuisinière poétique*, *Sur la Psychologie du goût*, and *Le Manuel culinaire aphrodisiaque, à l'usage des adultes des deux sexes.*

The recipes of this last book were said to heighten erotic powers, though Apollinaire did not need any assistance. According to the "manual," two recipes were particularly potent: a celery base and an artichoke purée cooked in salt, lemon, thick béchamel sauce, butter, and cream. He must have been on a strict diet of artichoke purée when he met Louise de Coligny-Châtillon—his *bien-aimée* in a lusty brief liaison: "Your breasts have a slight taste of persimmons and barbaric figs, / Your hips, candied fruit, I adore them, my darling." In Apollinaire's pigeon roost, it was literally one jump from the kitchen to the bed.

~~~~~~~~~~~~~~~~~~~~~~~

No making love now, my little chicken
Make us a good little meal.

—Apollinaire

In his relationship with painter Marie Laurencin, Apollinaire was the director and dictator of his crowded kitchen. Though he produced fabulous meals in his *cuisine-cabinet-de-toilette*, when poor Marie cooked, it was often the same simple meal of *saucisson*, risotto, and beef stew. According to Apollinaire, she was not gifted in the kitchen or in bed. One evening he gave her a good verbal thrashing over an ill-prepared risotto; at another soirée she was admonished for not being able to set the table properly. Yet their relationship lasted from 1907 to 1913—perhaps it was a poorly puffed soufflé that put an end to it all? He did find it in his heart to affectionately call Marie *mon sucre* in their more tender moments.

~~~~~~~~~~~~~~~~~~~~~~~~~~

She offers you two meals on a Sunday—enough food to make you ill—because everything is so delicious. Then she gives you full packets and baskets under each arm to take back on the last train to Paris.

—a Danish friend of Apollinaire

The first doggie bag may well have been invented by Angelica Kostrowicki, a gorgeous, rebellious, man-eating high roller of a woman—Apollinaire's mother. Daughter of a Polish count and an Italian woman, at sixteen Angelica was kicked out of her convent school, Collège des Dames françaises du Sacré Coeur, for bad behavior—an auspicious beginning for such a passionate, tyrannical, possessive, and authoritarian woman. Like her son, she was also an incredible gourmand. Poor as she was—and her finances depended largely on her luck at casinos—Angelica loved to cook and was inventive with the few ingredients that were available to her.

As her house was a crowded menagerie of bric-a-brac, furniture of all styles, dogs, a monkey, and a parrot, the kitchen was probably a haven for both her and her son. Apollinaire was proud of his mother's cooking and took great pleasure in sharing it with his friends. Though Angelica loved to feed Apollinaire, she was none too fond of these friends—uncouth, sloppy heathens living in the bowels of Paris. Commenting on her tempestuous and judgmental nature, Apollinaire wrote, "With my mother, it's always a malediction right away!" Still, despite her vehement disapproval of Apollinaire's companions, everyone who took the train out to Le Vésinet for Sunday lunch or dinner left her home with full stomachs and a remembrance of her: a doggie bag *à la française* filled with fresh ravioli, crusty bread, cornichons, fat plums in eau-de-vie, and apricot jam.

~~~~~~~~~~~~~~~~~~~~~~~~~~~

I've noticed . . . that people who know how to eat are never idiots.

—Apollinaire

When poet Max Jacob first met Apollinaire, he described his remarkable "terrible and brilliant hazelnut eyes [and Apollinaire's] tiny mouth like a pepper." If Apollinaire had been painted by the portraitist Giuseppe Arcimboldo, I think that each feature of the poet's face would be a meticulous rendering of a different food. Emerging from the somber background, his eyes rounded hazelnuts, his ears delicate candied fruits, his mouth a little red pepper, his eyebrows tiny oily anchovies, his cheeks plump sweet-smelling oranges, his nose a croissant, his neck thick rolls of country sausage tucked one upon another, and his hair powdered with inky spices. In the murky background, it would be difficult to distinguish his shadow from the dark pools of rich wines, from the silhouettes of lovers, poets, painters, singers. If you were to look closely enough, you would realize that the portrait was composed of thousands of minuscule letters in every possible color—each portion of his face really a poem, a word—capturing the perishable and the permanent in the puzzle of his face.

———

Apollinaire's love affair with food and drink lasted until his death at age thirty-eight in 1918 when, already weakened by a serious head injury from the First World War, he succumbed to the Spanish flu epidemic running rampant throughout Paris. Despite numerous complications caused by his head injury, Apollinaire continued to go out for meals, invite friends over for dinner, and regularly publish recipes in the *Mercure de France*. A few months before the poet's death, friend Maurice de Vlaminck wrote that "he still had his marvelous appetite and, at each dinner, devoured ham, partridge, and a half-bottle of brandy."

At this point in his life, the poet must have been a sight to see: a huge man staggering through the streets, holding court in cafés, devouring dish after dish with grease on his chin, winking at whores, laughing, drinking, smoking. At the same time, I think that Apollinaire was a fragile man—a small shadow slanting against the night-quiet Haussmann buildings, looking up beyond the mansard roofs to the distant sky, alone, out of breath.

~~~~~~~~~~~~~~~~~~~~~~~~~~~~~~~~

Last night in La Régalade, a cramped bistro tucked away in the 14th arrondissement, after the *terrine de campagne* and *petits cornichons fait maison* had been passed graciously from table to table, and as plate after plate of fantastic dishes flew by, I thought of Apollinaire. Food permeates his work—sometimes it is just a stanza, other times the main ingredient in a story, or simply a dash of dark liqueur to finish off a line of poetry. One gourmandise inspires another: his appetite for food cannot be separated from his appetite for words. Apollinaire wrote sensual, vivid, innovative poems, partly due to his profound appreciation for and love of food. His lush descriptions of women, the fragrant and stinking smells of Paris and its streets and markets and early mornings—these are palpable and poignant sensations in Apollinaire's work. He enjoyed indulging in evocative words and images, and, when reading his poems, I have no choice but to participate in the feast. To consider Apollinaire from the angle of the dinner table is to see an essential facet of his personality and his poetry, revealing a side that is fragile, mortal, and hungry.

RECIPE

Risotto with Piedmontese Truffles

This recipe was one of Apollinaire's preferred side dishes and can accompany seafood, beef, chicken, vegetables, etc. The secret to success is not to leave the risotto, not even for a minute, until it's completely cooked—and not a second more. (This last trick must have been poor Marie Laurencin's downfall . . .)

serves 6

INGREDIENTS:

1 ½ quarts beef or veal bouillon
1 pound Arborio rice
1 cup butter
1/8 pound raw chopped beef marrow
2 finely chopped shallots
1 finely chopped onion
2 or 3 raw white Piedmontese truffles, preferably with a
     garlic taste (or frankly any truffle, if you can't make it
     to Italy this weekend)
½–⅔ cup freshly grated Parmigiano-Reggiano cheese
A pinch of cayenne pepper

Carefully wash and dry the truffles, cut them into strips, and set them aside. In a saucepan, melt the butter on low heat and add the chopped onion, shallots, and beef marrow, then turn the heat up to medium. Add a pinch of cayenne pepper and be sure not to brown anything. Next, add the rice, mixing well and spreading it evenly throughout the saucepan. Add approximately ¼ cup of bouillon, stirring constantly at a low temperature. When the rice has absorbed all of the bouillon, continue to add ¼ cup at a time at a slow pace, making sure that no grains stick to the bottom of the pan. Continue stirring until all of the bouillon has been absorbed. Just before serving the risotto, add the truffles, and then sprinkle everything with freshly grated Parmesan cheese.

CONTRIBUTORS NOTES

STEVE ALMOND is the author of two story collections, *My Life in Heavy Metal* and *The Evil B. B. Chow,* and the nonfiction book *Candyfreak*. He lives and grills in Somerville, Massachusetts.

MATTHEW BATT's fiction and nonfiction have appeared in *Tin House, Another Chicago Magazine,* the *Isthmus, Soundings East, Western Humanities Review,* and elsewhere. He is an assistant professor of creative writing at Stephen F. Austin State University in Nacogdoches, Texas.

EUGENIA BONE has published articles in numerous newspapers and magazines, including *New York Magazine, Harper's Bazaar,* the *New York Times, Food & Wine,* and *Gourmet.* She is the author of two books: *At Mesa's Edge* and *Italian Family Dining,* written with her father, Edward Giobbi. She lives in New York and Colorado with her husband, architect Kevin Bone, and their two children, Carson and Mo.

LAN SAMANTHA CHANG is the author of a story collection, *Hunger,* and a novel, *Inheritance,* which won the 2005 PEN/ Beyond Margins Prize for the Novel. She lives in Iowa City, Iowa, where she teaches creative writing and directs the Iowa Writers' Workshop.

LYDIA DAVIS, a 2003 MacArthur Fellow, is the author of *Samuel Johnson Is Indignant*, *Almost No Memory*, *The End of the Story*, and *Break It Down*. Her work has appeared in *Harper's*, the *New Yorker*, *Bomb*, the *Paris Review*, *McSweeney's*, and elsewhere. Davis completed a highly acclaimed new translation of Marcel Proust's *Swann's Way* for Penguin Classics. Among other honors, she has been awarded a Guggenheim fellowship and a Lannan Literary Award. She lives in upstate New York with her family.

STUART DYBEK's most recent books are *I Sailed with Magellan*, a novel in stories, and *Streets in Their Own Ink*, poems, both published by Farrar, Straus and Giroux.

LISA GROSSMAN is a culinary and cultural historian and a frequent lecturer on the curious intersections of literature and gastronomy. She is a visiting professor at Long Island University and coauthor, with her late mother, of *Lobscouse & Spotted Dog*, the authorized Patrick O'Brian cookbook. She is currently at work on a translation of Marie-Antoine Carême's *L'Art de la cuisine française au XIX siècle*.

Born into a traditional family in Teheran, Iran, **SHUSHA GUPPY** moved to London in the 1960s. She is the author of *The Blindfold Horse*, which won the *Yorkshire Post* Book Award for best nonfiction book, a prize from the Royal Society of Literature, and the Grand Prix Littéraire de Elle, as well as *A Girl in Paris*,

Looking Back—A Panoramic View of a Literary Age, the travel book *Three Journeys in the Levant,* and *The Secret of Laughter—Folk-tales and Fairy-tales from Classical Persia*. For twenty years, until 2005, she was the London editor and a contributor to the *Paris Review*.

HEATHER HARTLEY's poems have appeared or are forthcoming in *Smartish Pace, Mississippi Review,* the *Los Angeles Review, Forklift Ohio, Kalliope,* and *Calyx,* among other publications. She is the Paris editor for *Tin House* magazine. She was awarded the first prize in poetry for the Tin House/Summer Literary Seminars in St. Petersburg, Russia, and her poems placed first in Brentano's Bookstore 2004 poetry contest (Paris). Her essays and interviews have appeared in *Web del Sol Review of Books* and *Naples Daily News* (Florida). She lives in Paris.

RICH KING, a former English teacher with the Portland, Oregon, public schools, currently lives and works in Manhattan as a consultant, promoter, and DJ in the fashion and nightlife industries. Looking to move beyond the difficulties New York faced in the beginning of the millennium, he became an active and determined participant in the rebuilding of the city's nightlife. When in New York, visit Rich at his ongoing weekly fêtes, SNAXX and BRUT: entertainment for men.

JEFF KOEHLER is the author of *La Paella: Deliciously Authentic Rice Dishes from Spain's Mediterranean Coast*. His writing about food and travel has appeared in numerous publications, including *Gourmet, Food & Wine, Eating Well,* the *Washington Post,* and the *Los Angeles Times.* He has also photographed two cookbooks, including Teresa Barrenechea's *The Cuisines of Spain,* which was a 2006 International Association of Culinary Professionals cookbook award finalist. After living in Africa, Asia, and London, he settled in Barcelona, where he has lived for most of the past ten years.

DAVID LEHMAN is the author of *When a Woman Loves a Man* (among other books of poems), the editor of *The Oxford Book of American Poetry,* and the series editor of *The Best American Poetry,* the annual anthology that he launched in 1988. He teaches in the graduate writing program at the New School in New York City.

CHRIS OFFUTT is the author of *Kentucky Straight, Out of the Woods, The Good Brother, The Same River Twice,* and *No Heroes.* His stories and essays have been published in *Esquire, GQ,* the *New York Times, Best American Short Stories,* and *Best Stories of the South.* He is the recipient of a Lannan Literary Award, a Whiting Writers' Award, a Guggenheim fellowship, an NEA grant, and a literature award from the American Academy of Arts and Letters for "prose that takes risks." His work is widely translated.

GRACE PALEY's books include *The Little Disturbances of Man,
Enormous Changes at the Last Minute, Later the Same Day,
Long Walks and Intimate Talks,* and *New and Collected Poems.*
Her stories have appeared in the *New Yorker, Mother Jones,*
and other magazines. She has taught at Columbia, Syracuse,
Sarah Lawrence, and City College. She has won a Guggenheim
fellowship, a National Institute of Arts and Letters Award for
short story writing, and was elected to the National Academy
of Arts and Letters. Born and raised in New York, she and her
husband live in Vermont.

SARA PERRY is a columnist for the *Oregonian* as well as a contributor to national publications and Web sites. She has written over a dozen cookbooks for Chronicle Books, including
*Holiday Baking, Everything Tastes Better with Bacon, The New
Complete Coffee Book,* and *Birthday Treats.* When she is not in
the kitchen (or at her computer), Sara has her nose in a book
or the latest issue of *Tin House.*

FRANCINE PROSE is the author of eleven novels, including *Blue
Angel,* which was nominated for a 2000 National Book Award.
Her most recent books are *A Changed Man,* a novel; *After,* a
novel for young adults; *Sicilian Odyssey,* a travel book; and *The
Lives of the Muses: Nine Women and the Artists They Inspired.* A
fellow of the New York Institute for the Humanities and a 1999
Director's Fellow of the New York Public Library's Center for
Scholars and Writers, she is a contributing editor to *Harper's*

and *Bomb* magazines and writes regularly on art for the *Wall Street Journal*.

A. J. RATHBUN's work has been published in a variety of national magazines, including *Crazyhorse*, *Gulf Coast*, the *Indiana Review*, the *Poetry Miscellany*, the *Sonora Review*, the *Southeast Review*, and *ZYZZYVA*, and he has been anthologized in *Pontoon: An Anthology of Washington Writers, Volumes III* and *V*. His books include *Want*, a poetry collection, and *Party Drinks*, a drink recipe collection.

SARA ROAHEN lives between New Orleans and Philadelphia. Her untitled book about falling in love with New Orleans through its food will be published by W. W. Norton in 2007.

LYNNE SAMPSON, a professional cook and baker, writes about food from her home in the Wallowa Mountains of northeastern Oregon. She has written for *Saveur*, *Fine Cooking*, the *Los Angeles Times*, and the *Washington Post* and was recently nominated for a James Beard journalism award.

ELISSA SCHAPPELL is the author of the novel *Use Me*; a contributing editor at *Vanity Fair*; a cofounder of *Tin House*, where she is now editor-at-large; a contributor to the *New York Times Book Review*; and coeditor with Jenny Offill of *The Friend Who Got Away* and the forthcoming *Money Changes Everything*.

CARLA SPARTOS is a senior editor at Zagat Survey. Her writings on food and drink have appeared in *New York Magazine* and the *Village Voice*. She lives in Brooklyn with her husband, Jim, and dog, Pierre.

MARK STATMAN's writing has appeared in many anthologies and journals, including *Tin House, Hanging Loose, The Hat, Bayou,* and *Conduit.* He is the author of *Listener in the Snow* and, with Christine McEwen, edited *The Alphabet of the Trees: A Guide to Nature Writing.* His translation (with Pablo Medina) of Garcia Lorca's *Poet in New York* is forthcoming from Grove Press. He is an associate professor of creative writing at Eugene Lang College.

ANTHONY SWOFFORD is the author of the memoir *Jarhead* and a forthcoming novel, *Exit A,* to be published in January of 2007, both from Scribner. He has taught at St. Mary's College and Lewis and Clark College. His awards include the PEN/Martha Albrand Award for the Art of the Memoir for *Jarhead* and a James Michener/Copernicus Society fellowship. He lives in New York City.

MICHELLE WILDGEN is the author of a novel, *You're Not You,* and a senior editor at *Tin House.* Her work has appeared in the anthologies *Best New American Voices 2004, Best Food Writing 2004, Death by Pad Thai and Other Unforgettable Meals,* and in literary magazines such as *StoryQuarterly, TriQuarterly, Prairie Schooner,* and elsewhere.

COPYRIGHT NOTES